Stephen Chambers

1991

—

SATHER CLASSICAL LECTURES

Volume Fifty-three

An Archaeology of Greece

An Archaeology of Greece

THE PRESENT STATE
AND FUTURE SCOPE
OF A DISCIPLINE

Anthony M. Snodgrass

University of California Press

BERKELEY · LOS ANGELES · LONDON

University of California Press
Berkeley and Los Angeles, California

University of California Press, Ltd.
London, England

© 1987 by
The Regents of the University of California

Library of Congress Cataloging-in-Publication Data

Snodgrass, Anthony M.
   An archaeology of Greece.
   (Sather classical lectures; v. 53)
   Includes index.
   1. Greece—Antiquities.   2. Archaeology—Greece.
I. Title.   II. Series.
DF77.S49   1987   938   86-19702
ISBN 0-520-05885-0 (alk. paper)

Printed in the United States of America

1 2 3 4 5 6 7 8 9

Maria Künzl zum Gedenken

Contents

Acknowledgments

Many acknowledgments conclude by thanking friends without whose assistance the book would never have been finished. I must begin with the admission that but for certain friends' initiative, this book would never have been started. My first and deepest debt is to the Sather Committee and the Department of Classics of the University of California, Berkeley, who, in inviting me to give the Sather Classical Lectures for 1984/85, made me the kind of offer that, whatever the trepidation it induces, one does not refuse. The invitation came with several years' notice; yet despite some feverish thought over the intervening period about what I should say, I arrived in California in late August 1984 in a state of unpreparedness. It was then that I needed, and received, the unstinting encouragement of friends on all sides, among whom I must single out the chairman of the department, Leslie Threatte, together with Jock Anderson, Crawford Greenewalt, Andrew Stewart, and Ronald Stroud. Presently I was joined by my wife Annemarie, who had just suffered the heaviest of blows in the death of her much-loved mother, Maria Künzl, but who also provided whole-hearted support at a critical stage. The benevolent climate of Berkeley, both literal and figurative, did the rest: the warm hospitality of colleagues in and beyond the Department of Classics and the stimulus given by the students in my graduate class were constantly inspiriting, and I benefited from the encouragement of lecture and seminar audiences in Santa Cruz, Stanford, San Jose, Davis, Los Angeles, Malibu, and Vancouver and Victoria, B.C. I had also enjoyed a helpful correspondence with Lucia Nixon in Athens, some of whose fruits have materialized in the opening pages of chapter 4; and I would single out the special generosity of Hamish Forbes, Hans-Volkmar Herrmann, and Mervyn Popham, who have allowed me to reproduce here versions of plans not previously published.

To these acknowledgments I must add a sincere expression of gratitude to the Deutsches Archäologisches Institut, Berlin, and its President, Prof. Dr. Edmund Buchner, whose generous hospitality in the spring of 1985 gave me a precious month of leisure, unavailable in Berkeley and unthinkable in Cambridge, to set about writing a final draft of the book. To all of them, and to many other colleagues in Cambridge, California, Paris, and Berlin with whom I discussed some of the ideas here presented, I owe a debt greater than any that this book could discharge.

A. M. SNODGRASS

Cambridge,
June 1985

List of Abbreviations

AA	*Archäologischer Anzeiger*
ABV	J. D. Beazley, *Attic Black-figure Vase Painters* (Oxford: Clarendon Press, 1956)
AJA	*American Journal of Archaeology*
AM	*Mitteilungen des Deutschen Archäologischen Instituts, Athenische Abteilung*
Annuario	*Annuario della Scuola Archeologica di Atene*
Ant. K.	*Antike Kunst*
BASOR	*Bulletin of the American Schools of Oriental Research*
BCH	*Bulletin de Correspondance Hellénique*
BSA	*Annual of the British School at Athens*
CAH	*Cambridge Ancient History, 2nd edition* (Cambridge: Cambridge University Press, 1970–)
CRAI	*Comptes-rendus de l'Académie des Inscriptions et Belles-Lettres*
IG	*Inscriptiones Graecae* (Berlin: G. Reiner, W. de Gruyter, 1873–)
Jahrb. RGZM	*Jahrbuch des Römisch-Germanischen Zentralmuseums Mainz*

JFA	*Journal of Field Archaeology*
JHS	*Journal of Hellenic Studies*
MEFR	*Mélanges d'Archéologie et d'Histoire publiés par l'Ecole française de Rome*
PCPS	*Proceedings of the Cambridge Philological Society*
PdP	*La Parola del Passato*
RA	*Revue Archéologique*
REG	*Revue des Etudes Grecques*
Rh.Mus	*Rheinisches Museum*
RM	*Mitteilungen des Deutschen Archäologischen Instituts, Römische Abteilung*
SMEA	*Studi micenei ed egeo-anatolici*
TAPA	*Transactions of the American Philological Association*

Foreword

"Archaeology," wrote Sterling Dow twenty years ago of the appointments to the Sather Professorship, "has been more or less consciously avoided. . . . Archaeology studied for itself is represented solely by J. D. Beazley."[1] This latter judgment implied that Dow excluded from such a description his own tenure, and that of others, such as A. W. Persson, in earlier years. Since he wrote, there has of course been Emily Vermeule's notable occupancy of the professorship in 1974/75, which would certainly come under the rubric of "archaeology studied for itself," even though she also handled literary evidence in a depth that I shall prove unable to match. But the fact remains that thirty-five years elapsed from the first Sather Lectures to Beazley's tenure; a further twenty-six between Beazley and Vermeule; and to the present only a further ten. This diminishing interval seems to me to reflect a growing awareness of the potential contribution of classical archaeology to classical studies, rather than being any kind of tribute to the greater distinction with which the discipline has recently been practiced; and the burden of responsibility laid on the archaeological incumbents is likewise surely enhanced by their rarity.

Such assumptions, whether well-founded or no, lead directly

1. S. Dow, *Fifty Years of Sathers* (Berkeley and Los Angeles, 1965), 47.

to the initial questions I wish to pose. How well equipped is the discipline of classical archaeology to play this putative larger role in the future of classical studies? How deserving is it of the honor of having one of its practitioners invited to hold the Sather Professorship in the mid 1980s? How high, in short, is its current and potential intellectual standing? What follows here will hardly constitute even the basis of an answer to such questions. I should remind you that, by my title and by my competence, I am confined to Greek archaeology, and, although I shall make intermittent reference to Roman and Italian archaeology, I do not wish my generalizations, and especially my criticisms, to be taken to apply to those fields. I should also make it clear that I do not include in my definition of archaeology the sister disciplines of epigraphy and numismatics. Of these subjects, indeed, it might to some extent be claimed that they are already practicing what I shall here be preaching.

Still, anyone who uses such a presumptuous-sounding title as mine—despite the studied use of the indefinite article—owes his readers some further explanation. By what authority do I imply (and I do mean so to imply) that there is room for a different approach to the archaeology of Greece from that traditionally and currently adopted? Do I seriously intend to advance here a full program for such an approach, in the fond hope that someone will follow it? In fact, my aims are both less and greater than this: less, in that I shall try, not to be programmatic, but to exemplify; and in that I freely acknowledge that many other "archaeologies of Greece," of at least equal validity, could be devised; but also greater, in that I shall not stop at mere advocacy. I honestly believe, not only that there is room for alternative approaches, but that the force of practical circumstances in Greece will eventually compel the adoption of a major change in our priorities in the subject, whether we are Greeks or foreigners.

(These practical considerations will emerge in chapter 4.) Since it is better to embrace innovation from choice, rather than having it thrust upon one, I shall try throughout to emphasize some of the positive reasons why change might be desirable.

(*Note*: Translations are the author's unless otherwise stated.)

CHAPTER ONE

The Health of a Discipline

DIE ARCHÄOLOGIE IST IM GRUNDE
EINE NAIVE WISSENSCHAFT.
W.-H. Schuchhardt, *Adolf Furtwängler* (1956)

M any of the more thoughtful professional expo-
nents of archaeology in the present generation have been troubled by the suggestion
that they practice a "naive science." A good number have joined
in the active search for changes to raise the intellectual standing
of their discipline. Few of this number, however, have been classical archaeologists; and this is merely a recent and relatively
conspicuous sign of a long-standing, and long-accepted, state of
affairs.

Elementary grammar might suggest that "classical archaeology" is a subdiscipline that forms an integral part of one subject
—archaeology—and has especially close links with another—
classics. But elementary grammar, here as in some other instances, is profoundly misleading. In the first place, it obscures
the fact that, operationally speaking, classical archaeology is
more closely linked to a third discipline, art history, than it is to
either archaeology or classics. That is to say, research and teaching connected with the history of Greek and Roman art have ac-
counted for a very large proportion of the activities, over the past
two hundred years, of those called classical archaeologists. Even
now, more than half of the sum of their work must be of this kind.

But, secondly, when we turn from the operational to the *institutional* aspect, the realities again give the lie to grammar: for we find that classical archaeologists, if they work in universities, are much more often grouped formally with classicists than with archaeologists, or for that matter with art historians, though there are exceptions.

It is not difficult to discern the accidental historical factors—the extraordinary artistic attainments of the Greeks and Romans in the first case, the educational background of the individual classical archaeologist in the second—that explain these apparent discrepancies. If it were merely a question of nomenclature, one could point to many other academic subjects that, at least in older universities, sometimes retain names—from "Physic" and "Natural History" to "Rhetoric"—that once corresponded both to real activities and to contemporary linguistic practice for describing those activities; but that have been rendered misleading by subsequent developments in one or both respects. But I do not believe that classical archaeology is in quite the same position as these other subjects, or that the issue *is*, in its case, purely one of nomenclature. Rather, I would argue, many classical archaeologists are to this day consciously or unconsciously pursuing, albeit in a more organized way, the same objectives as the founding father of their discipline, Johann Joachim Winckelmann, dead now for more than two hundred years. Likewise, the normal institutional arrangement within universities reflects the hard fact that the published results of the activity of classical archaeologists, where their interest extends beyond the confines of the subject itself, are more likely to be read and used by classicists than by the practitioners of archaeology, art history, or any other subject.

But from these preliminaries, we come now to a somewhat paradoxical conclusion. Grammar and nomenclature, operational and institutional practice may all unite in implying that classical archaeology is a dependent subsidiary of some other subject; yet in a way that implication is false. The fact is that the traditional activities of classical archaeologists do not today conform at all closely to those of any other discipline. To this extent—and herein lies the paradox—classical archaeology *is* an independent subject.

The reasons for this qualified independence, as so far considered, are negative ones: the subject is tradition-bound and it lacks wide academic appeal. Of the three adjacent disciplines that have come under discussion, two at least have passed through a period of change, or at least of ferment: there are today both a new archaeology and a new art history. Both these new movements have gained considerable ground within their subjects; but in so doing, they have had the effect of carrying those subjects further away from any contact with classical archaeology.

This has not been an encouraging introduction, and it is time to say something more positive. If one of the messages of this book is that even the present degree of qualified independence retained by classical archaeology should be given up, this will not, I think, prove to be a major sacrifice; certainly not in proportion to the potential gains. What I believe is that the present dignified remoteness of the subject on the academic plane could give way to the kind of acknowledged intellectual vitality that attracts attention across a range of other disciplines. If this happens, I believe that classical archaeology will still be found to be an exceptional discipline; but exceptional in its capacity to contribute to the fulfillment of new aims rather than in its fidelity to old ones. I think that classical archaeology can answer some of the more pressing needs of the new movement in archaeology, and that its capacity to integrate ancient art history into the study of the total material culture of the classical civilizations opens the way to a kind of art-historical approach that is often impossible in the case of other epochs. This broadening of range would undoubtedly also increase the potential participation of classical archaeology in the work of the other branches of classical studies.

Since classical archaeology's closest relationship is with classics, it is worth taking a slightly closer look at the present nature of this relationship. Some classical archaeologists would accept their traditional grouping within classics without question, and under pressure many more would on balance settle for a continuation of that arrangement. But it is harder to elicit true candor as to how classicists regard classical archaeology, and I want to try to consider this topic without relapsing into anecdotalism. There are certain considerations that are more obviously relevant to the British university system than to any other, but that may nevertheless deserve mention. First, it is not only possible but relatively common in Britain to achieve a degree in classics, even an outstanding degree, without having devoted one hour's study to classical archaeology. Second, to broach more delicate matters, it is also quite common for a very moderate undergraduate performance in classics to be the prelude to a specialized career in classical archaeology. This second observation loses much of its significance if, as many would maintain, classical archaeology requires quite different skills from pure classics; and both points depend for their importance on the degree to which the British pattern is matched in other countries.

At this point, however, objective criteria begin to run out, and I fall back on my subjective impressions, formed by experience of three very different British universities, and refined by briefer encounters with a number of institutions in other countries. I hazard the generalization that the repute of classical archaeology as a discipline has, in the past, been a fairly modest one among other classicists; but that the situation is today slowly improving. Scholars in other branches of classical studies seem increasingly to be acknowledging the relevance of material and physical evidence to their own researches: this happens occasionally among ancient philosophers, sporadically among philologists, more frequently among literary scholars, and most prominently among ancient historians. The realization leads to increasingly frequent consultation of classical archaeologists, either through the medium of the latter's writings or directly and orally. The first often precedes the second, a sign perhaps of some discrepancy in objectives, or else in linguistic codes. The results are seen when the classicist in question handles such matters in print. Though one can still find examples of the absolute disclaimer—a declaration of total abstention from archaeology—even in connection with topics where archaeological evidence could obviously be applied, the mere inclusion of such a statement (as opposed to complete silence) may be taken as a sign of advance. More often nowadays one finds the classicist bringing at least a bold pair of tongs to a topic for which there is relevant archaeological material, and a polite note of acknowledgment to an archaeologist will be included. To tell the truth, the archaeologist in question is sometimes the one whose office is just along the corridor, who is charitably assumed to have a mastery of his whole subject. But there has been a detectable move away from the tone of lofty disdain once in order for such citations: the tone of, say, the judge proudly disowning all knowledge of vaudeville has given place to that of the father excusing himself to his children for his ignorance of pop music. Sometimes the degree of commitment expressed is much greater than this, however; and, best of all, some classicists today are prepared to familiarize themselves at first hand with archaeological material, and with what has been written about it.

The severest test undoubtedly comes when issues arise where the archaeological and the literary or documentary evidence are in conflict. In these contexts, one can still hear (if not read) unabashed statements as to the virtual worthlessness of the former class of evidence. Surprising though it may seem, my own treatment of a few such issues in the second chapter of this book might be read as giving a measure of support to such attitudes, though not to their expression in this form. But all the reactions that we have been surveying are alike in that they at least imply recognition of some kind. They may not, most of them, be compatible with a view of classical archaeology as a central and indispensable adjunct of classical learning; but they show an acknowledgment that this allied subject exists, and that its practitioners are people who can understand one's own language and can on occasion be consulted with advantage. Furthermore, as I have suggested, the relationship between pure classics and classical archaeology is improving today, at least in some superficial ways.

Even if accepted in full, these statements may not appear to add up to much—even when one adds to them the observation, made in my Foreword, that the appointment of archaeologists to the Sather Professorship of Classical Literature has apparently come to seem progressively less incongruous in recent decades. But all this appears in a different light once one turns, by way of comparison, to the relationship between classical and nonclassical archaeology.

The intellectual revolution within nonclassical archaeology has gone a long way towards transforming the nature of that discipline. Most nonclassical archaeologists in America and Britain, a good many in France, Italy, and Scandinavia, and a few in Germany and Eastern Europe may be reckoned among its supporters. The revolutionary movement cannot keep forever the title it has adopted, but "new archaeology" is still a recognizable and perhaps an acceptable appellation in the 1980s. The impact of the new archaeology has had many beneficial effects, and even if it had not, its great following would make it a force to be reckoned with. Some of the approaches and methods of the new movement seem to cry out for application in the classical context; classical archaeology for its part stands in some need of the stimulus this would bring; but so far, from the point of view of the narrow interests of classical archaeology *sensu stricto*, the advent of the new movement in archaeology has been something of a disaster. To be criticized, even attacked, is one thing; to have the very existence of one's subject ignored is another.[1]

There are reasons for this silence, both obvious and underlying. In America, for one thing, much of the literature of the new archaeology, whether prehistoric or historical in content, is North American not only in authorship but in subject matter. Of course, this explanation can hardly be applied to Europe. There, the most influential single figure has without doubt been David Clarke (1937–76).[2] I may be prejudiced in favor of a fellow archaeologist whom I knew and liked, but with Clarke I always felt that a door to classical archaeology was kept slightly ajar. In his best-known work, *Analytical Archaeology*, he admitted evidence from two areas that, though they lie respectively on the edge of, and within, classical archaeology, have always been "privileged fields" among British new archaeologists: the Aegean Bronze Age and Roman Britain. It is true that in the thirteen-page index to the second (posthumous) edition of that book, all mention of key terms such as "Aegean," "Roman," "obsidian," "spondylus," and "Dressel type 1 amphorae" has been extirpated, as if somehow impure; but the discussions are still there, and can be found by those who know enough to look instead for key concepts such as "distance decay models," or key names such as "Hodder, I." and "Renfrew, C." On the other hand, Clarke's next major work, the essays he edited under the title *Models in Archaeology*, offered twenty-five contributions of which not a single one dealt with the Mediterranean world in any period later than the pre-

---

1. See, in this connection, A. M. Snodgrass, "The New Archaeology and the Classical Archaeologist," *AJA* 89 (1985): 31–37, a paper presented at a meeting of the Archaeological Institute of America, New York, April 3, 1984.

2. See, especially, his *Analytical Archaeology* (London, 1968; 2nd ed. 1978, ed. R. Chapman), and the posthumous *Analytical Archaeologist*, edited by his colleagues (London, 1978). For tributes to the man, see, for example, (G. E. Daniel) *Antiquity* 50 (1976): 183–84, and B. Wailes, "David L. Clarke," *JFA* 4 (1977): 133–34.

historic.[3] Less often noted is the olive branch he held out in a short, but important, article to archaeologists working on the better-documented cultures: their studies would, he wrote, "provide vital experiments" in using the control of documentary sources over inferences based on purely material evidence.[4] This procedure is, as we shall find in the next chapter, roughly the converse of what traditional classical archaeology has spent part of its time doing. But in any case David Clarke's tragically early death not long after had a dampening effect on whatever initiatives he had in mind here, as indeed on archaeological endeavor of many kinds. His successors have shown little interest either in taking up those initiatives themselves or in monitoring the activities of those already working in these other branches of archaeology. This absence of communication was certainly not characteristic of the work of the previous generation of nonclassical archaeologists: read the writings of Gordon Childe, Christopher Hawkes, or Stuart Piggott and you will find, not only rich evidence of communication with classical (and other "historical") archaeologists, but also learned and firsthand familiarity with their subject matter. This is why I said earlier that, in this direction, the outward relationships of classical archaeology actually appear to be weakening.

One can find explanations for the change at several deeper levels. There is, first of all, an almost technical factor: since many of the theoretical models now adopted in European prehistory are ones that sternly exclude the possibility of links with the classical world contributing to cultural change, it naturally follows that familiarity with the material of classical archaeology has less claim to attention. On a more abstract level, most younger archaeologists today, in Europe almost as much as in America, see

3. As was observed by J.-C. Gardin, "A propos des modèles en archéologie," *RA* (1974), pt. 2, 341–48.
4. D.L. Clarke, "Archaeology: The Loss of Innocence," *Antiquity* 47 (1973): 18.

their subject as having more in common with anthropology than with a historical and linguistic discipline such as classics. A conspicuous by-product of this reorientation has been the language barrier that has grown up between the younger new archaeologists and more traditionally minded practitioners of their own and other disciplines. David Clarke made this into a substantive issue by advocating the use of what he called "interconnecting jargon."[5] Ironically, he meant this as a way of building bridges across interdisciplinary gulfs, but he did not have this particular gulf in mind.

I am not going to add to the volumes of (usually rather angry) discussion that have been expended on the linguistic style of the new archaeology, but turn instead to an allied, but slightly different, question—that of linguistic genre. It struck me recently that, when Jeremy Sabloff was invited to contribute a survey of intellectual trends in American archaeology, he could not have chosen a better phrase than he did for his main title: "When the Rhetoric Fades."[6] When advocacy predominates, as it has done so far in the literature of the new archaeology, at the expense of exemplification and practice in general, the existence is implied of a larger audience of colleagues whose main role is to be convinced by that advocacy. The most valid criticism of the new archaeology is surely that, to date, it has preached too much and practiced too little. I am reminded of the (no doubt apocryphal) social worker who said: "We are all here on earth to help others; what on earth the others are here for, I don't know."

Finally, there is an explanation at a deeper psychological level for the estrangement between classical archaeology and the "new archaeology." It is to be found in the categorization of human intellects. I was first alerted to the existence of a possible scien-

5. D. L. Clarke, ed., *Models in Archaeology* (London, 1972), 75.
6. "When the Rhetoric Fades: a Brief Appraisal of Intellectual Trends in American Archaeology During the Past Two Decades," *BASOR* 242 (Spring 1981): 1–6.

tific basis for making a distinction between "convergent" and "divergent" types of intellect by Liam Hudson's *Contrary Imaginations.*[7] Hudson distinguishes between the convergent type of mind, which excels at finding the right answer to questions where there *is* a right answer, and the divergent type, which excels in the quite different aptitude for thinking of a wide variety of possible answers to questions that are open-ended. The two types were found to correlate with different ranges of academic subjects chosen for specialization. The group Hudson studied consisted of fairly intelligent boys at English secondary schools, and this limitation may appear to invite obvious criticism: for example, on grounds of the exclusion of girls, or of the restriction in specialization to subjects offered in English secondary schools. But Hudson's results showed an impressive consistency. At the converger end of the scale—that is to say, among those whose intelligence showed a marked bias towards success in solving the "right answer" problems and relative weakness in the open-ended tests—it was the future specialists in mathematics, physics, chemistry, and—alone among arts subjects—classics, who featured prominently. At the opposing, diverger end of the spectrum, history, English literature, and modern languages were common choices. There are also a few pieces of evidence scattered through Hudson's book to suggest that the future practitioners of archaeology in general, had they been a clearly identifiable group, would also have featured at the divergent end—an impression reinforced by many public pronouncements of the new archaeologists (on the undesirability of particularism and empiricism, for example), notwithstanding their advocacy of scientific method. It is not, then, surprising that some of the sharp-

7. Liam Hudson, *Contrary Imaginations* (London, 1966). For the connection between mentality and choice of subject, see 42 and 157, table 3. For hints of a correlation between "divergence" and an interest in archaeology, 26–27 (the maverick biologist "Wernick") and 157 n. 4 (an extreme diverger); see, generally, 146 for the finding of "rebelliousness" among social scientists.

est mutual criticism in the academic world, between or within disciplines, comes from the opposing ends of this spectrum. It is hardly a coincidence, for example, that the one full-length critique of the new archaeology that has so far appeared has come from within classical archaeology—Paul Courbin's *Qu'est-ce que l'archéologie?*[8]—or that its criticism should be predominantly unfavorable. Archaeology is in the unusual (though not necessarily unfortunate) position that the extremes of convergence and divergence can be predicted to occur within the same discipline—or at least, in a discipline that goes by a single name—and it is not so far obvious that the results of this tension have been beneficial. Complementary endeavor and fruitful rivalry require a higher degree of mutual respect than the two sides in this dichotomy have hitherto been able to muster.

There are, in short, a variety of reasons why a neglect of classical archaeology, on the part of the new archaeologists especially, was predictable. But how far was it also justifiable? Some would perhaps embark on a simple quantitative line of reasoning here. If pursued to its logical conclusion, this would presumably run as follows: "Classical archaeology deals with cultures that, at their mean spatial extent, covered perhaps 5 percent of the inhabited surface of the globe and, in temporal duration, comprise perhaps .04 of 1 percent of man's existence to date: *ergo*, it merits the attention of .00002, or one in 50,000, of the world's archaeologists, or the same proportion of the time of all of them." This is, of course, a *reductio ad absurdum*, as everyone would acknowledge: and the reasons for this realization are not without relevance. They range from considerations of the past—the differential speed of human cultural advance—to those of the present—the state of our existing knowledge—and to those that link present and past—the legacy of classical civilization to modern thought and practice. I choose these examples because they can

---

8. P. Courbin, *Qu'est-ce que l'archéologie?* (Paris, 1982).

in some measure claim to be objectively measurable; arguments that cannot make such a claim (aesthetic admiration, pedagogic value, sheer interest) are best passed over here.

The crude quantitative argument is clearly not a clinching one, but other arguments might be advanced. If it is at all true that classical archaeology suffers from a "separation from a common tradition of archaeological research," that it has "painted itself into a corner" (I borrow both these phrases from other, more or less worried, commentators within the subject), then there are grounds for anxiety that extend far beyond the lack of communication with the new archaeology. Classical archaeology may excel in offering strikingly new answers to old questions; but in the long run this is much less fruitful than asking entirely new questions. A healthy discipline is one where major advances occur from time to time in the way the subject is practiced, and, as a result, in the kind of work people actually do. I would judge that this is true of most intellectually vital disciplines today, and furthermore that the frequency of these "breakthroughs" has perceptibly increased in the second half of the twentieth century, thanks no doubt to improved communications and an increase in the total input of time and money. Classical archaeology has benefited, if more modestly than many subjects, from these favorable factors of recent years; yet, as adumbrated in the opening pages of this book, it cannot easily point to major advances and reorientations of thought.

Another test of the health of a discipline was also hinted at earlier: its capacity to maintain a balanced, bilateral relationship with other, superficially entirely distinct, subjects. For archaeology as a whole, David Clarke in 1972 advocated an attitude that "allows the possibility that archaeology can make outward contributions to other disciplines, *an essential feature if the discipline is to survive*" (my emphasis). He claimed that (again, for archaeology as a whole) such outward contribution had already begun on a small scale "towards branches of mathematics, computer studies and classification, and to the social and behavioral sciences."[9] He was doubtless right, but most archaeologists would certainly admit that archaeology's intellectual "balance of trade" with other subjects remains markedly in deficit; and in any case, what contribution has classical archaeology made on the outgoing side? One could easily point to fruitful, two-way collaborations between classical studies in general and other disciplines; for example, with anthropology, as the Sather Lectures of E. R. Dodds thirty-five years ago, and of Geoffrey Kirk and Walter Burkert more recently, serve to remind us;[10] but for much of this period, classical *archaeology* as such hardly participated in the collaboration. The beginnings of a major, archaeologically based contribution to anthropology (within the classical field, that is) may be perceptible in the work of the school emanating from the Centre de Recherches Comparées dans les Sociétés anciennes in Paris,[11] which will make other calls on our attention later on.

Perhaps we have reached a point where it may be conceded, at least for the purposes of the argument, that classical archaeology today stands in danger of a certain stultification. If so, the explanation may partly lie in its traditional incorporation in classical studies, and in its resultant tendency to accept aims originally laid down for it by the sister subjects of classics and ancient history. I would argue that classical archaeology has an existence as a branch of knowledge independent of even these allied disciplines; and this argument seems to lead inexorably to the conclu-

9. Clarke, ed., *Models in Archaeology* (cited above, n. 5), 75.

10. See E. R. Dodds, *The Greeks and the Irrational*; G. S. Kirk, *Myth: Its Meaning and Functions in Ancient and Other Cultures*; and W. Burkert, *Structure and History in Greek Mythology and Ritual* (Berkeley and Los Angeles, 1951, 1970, and 1979, respectively vols. 25, 40, and 47 of the Sather Classical Lectures).

11. An early landmark here was the 1977 colloquium in Ischia published as *La Mort, les morts dans les sociétés anciennes*, ed. G. Gnoli and J.-P Vernant (Cambridge, 1982), where both the organizers (A. Schnapp and B. d'Agostino) and more than half the contributors were archaeologists.

sion that that existence should lie within archaeology as a whole, since the alternative has been seen to be a rather sterile isolation (see above, pp. 2–3). If it is to achieve the intellectual vitalization that I believe lies within its grasp, then it can only do so by capitalizing on its own strengths. These derive from factors and achievements that on the one hand are really quite independent of its traditional subordination to classical studies and on the other exempt it from the need merely to ape the practices of other branches of archaeology.

Classical archaeology has many strengths, whether potential or realized. It cannot, for example, be entirely without interest for archaeologists of any persuasion that there exists a branch of their subject where it is possible for the results of fieldwork, not merely to show the empirical plausibility of, but conclusively to verify earlier hypotheses; and we shall see presently that classical archaeology has such a capacity. More prosaically, classical archaeology can dispose of a body of evidence that is notable, not only for its sheer quantity, but for the degree of "processing" it has already undergone. There is in the first place a relatively strong tradition of full publication of excavation finds and museum collections, a point rightly emphasized by Colin Renfrew in his centennial address to the Archaeological Institute of America in 1980,[12] though he was tactful enough not to spell out the implied contrast with the record of other branches of archaeology in this respect. The phrase "The Great Tradition," which Renfrew used in his title on that occasion, was I think intended to apply first and foremost to classical archaeology, and to reflect "greatness" in a wider field than that of mere thoroughness in the publishing of results.

Let us however consider a small example of how this specific tradition of full publication might be turned to fruitful use. Among other things, the new archaeology advocates building up

12. "The Great Tradition Versus the Great Divide," *AJA* 84 (1980): 287–98, especially 295.

"a body of central theory capable of synthesizing the general regularities within its data."[13] In *Method and Theory in Historical Archaeology* (another work, incidentally, that despite its title mentions classical archaeology only as a kind of type-symbol), Stanley South observes such a general regularity in the shape of a patterned casting-off of behavioral by-products around an occupation-site, naming it the Carolina Artifact Pattern.[14] This was abstracted from five separate excavated deposits of eighteenth-century date, each on about the scale of a single domestic unit, dug by himself or another excavator in North and South Carolina between 1960 and 1973. Having established the existence of this pattern, he rightly sought to test its validity and extent by comparing the data from other sites of the period within the area then dominated by British colonial culture—only to discover that such data were difficult to find: other excavators had not provided complete artifact lists. Eventually he found one adequately published site, Signal Hill in Newfoundland, which offered for comparison three deposits of slightly later date (c. 1800–1860). But even here there was a difficulty: the excavator had not listed nails (a detail that touched the heart of a reader who, intermittently over the past twenty years, has been saddled with the responsibility for publishing iron nails from Mediterranean excavations). South had to extrapolate a ratio of numbers of nails to total numbers of all finds in the "Architectural" classification, before he could proceed with the testing (whose results indeed proved positive) of the Carolina Artifact Pattern.

Let us imagine, however, that South had elected to carry out his study, not in colonial North America, but in classical Greece. What he would then have found is that one site alone, Olynthus, would have provided over eighty assemblages, each on the scale of a single domestic unit, with finds of a variety of types recorded

13. Clarke, *Analytical Archaeology* (cited above, n. 2), xv.
14. S. South, *Method and Theory in Historical Archaeology* (New York, 1977), chap. 4.

by location.[15] It is also significant that these deposits, excavated between 1928 and 1938, were (notwithstanding the intervention of a world war and enemy occupation of the site) fully published by 1952, in fourteen volumes, nails and all. I hope this first point is sufficiently clearly made.

Classical archaeology can certainly boast a "Great Tradition" in works of synthesis and analysis, especially in the essentially visual branch of the subject. The two greatest names here are undoubtedly those of Adolf Furtwängler (1853–1907) and Sir John Beazley (1885–1970). Both men had the extraordinary capacity of looking at thousands, indeed tens of thousands, of archaeological objects of a given kind and, at least for a critical period, retaining some kind of memory of every one of them. Take, for example, the work that was probably Furtwängler's masterpiece, *Die griechischen Gemmen* (1900): we learn from Schuchhardt's commemorative lecture, which provides the epigraph to this chapter, that in the writing of this book, Furtwängler examined between fifty and sixty thousand engraved stones. As for Beazley, in his two major works on Athenian painted pottery alone, he classified and attributed some thirty thousand of these larger and more elaborately decorated objects. In so doing, each man systematically organized and established the pattern for a whole subbranch of archaeology. That they did so "for all time" (as Schuchhardt tentatively claimed for Furtwängler's work on gems) is not necessarily to be accepted, or indeed wished for. It is an admirable feature of many academic disciplines (though one that occasionally generates stress) that they combine unswerving loyalty to past heroes with the realization that the future vitality of the subject depends in part on the fallibility of these same figures.

15. See D. M. Robinson, *Excavations at Olynthus*, vol. 14, *Terracotta and Lamps Found in 1934 and 1938* (Baltimore, 1952), "Master Concordance of Proveniences," 465–510, supplementing the "Concordance of Proveniences" for metal finds and loom-weights in vol. 10 (1941), 535–50, and replacing earlier partial concordances in vols. 8 (1938), 344–54, and 13 (1950), 451–53.

Thus it is easy to anticipate the lines of criticism to which even such works as these are vulnerable. With Beazley, for example (much more than with Furtwängler), there is the serious point that in general he abstained from setting out the steps of reasoning that led him to his attributions of vases, being largely content to let the results speak for themselves. One recalls another plea from the preface of *Analytical Archaeology*: for "systematic and ordered study based upon clearly defined models and rules of procedure." In a similar way, it is undeniable that many classical excavation reports are content to follow a time-honored routine in the presentation of their finds, rather than to explain or modify that routine.

Yet another aspect of classical archaeology's "Great Tradition"—this time unquestionably a by-product of its association with the other branches of classical studies—is an almost unique degree of acquaintance with the topography and history of its own archaeological terrain. This applies not only to the territory of Greece and Italy, but in some degree to that of every one of the twenty-five or so other modern countries that, at some period, lay partly or wholly within the cultural orbit of Greece and Rome. One can put one's finger where one chooses on a large-scale map of any relevant part of Europe, Asia, or Africa: the chances are that someone, somewhere would be able to give you a fair idea of what was happening in that specific area two thousand years ago. Can as much be said of any other area, of remotely comparable size, in the world?

But this boast, once again, is not one that brings all discussion to an end. The local museum director who knows everything about the archaeology of the province of Monsalvat or Münchhausen may well have a mastery of the two classical cultures that enables him to carry out effective fieldwork in some quite distant part of the classical world—say Roman North Africa. Conversely, he may well have skills that qualify him to excavate, say, a prehistoric burial or a late medieval abbey (as well as a classical

site), as long as they are in his own province. But both his time
range and his space range, though they may be quite great in the
one dimension, are small in the other. He will be unusual if he
has knowledge of, or interest in, the general archaeological principles that would enable him to fill the intervening gaps and
transform his two intersecting furrows into a rationally culti-
vated field. Unless he has, he can hardly without qualification be
called an "archaeologist."

It is in fact to archaeological fieldwork that I wish to devote
the remainder of this chapter. The claim that classical archaeology has a "Great Tradition" here as well will probably be widely
received with raucous laughter in other archaeological circles, so
low has its repute sunk in this respect. Yet it was once a reasonable claim, and perhaps not so long ago as many would imagine.
I wish to give some examples that will show some of the distinctive strengths of classical archaeology in terms where all can assess them, though I hope also not to shrink from acknowledging
the limitations that these examples reveal. They will, I hope,
serve to make clear one of the reasons why I think classical archaeology has a unique contribution to make to the advance-
ment of archaeological practice.

I begin, perhaps unexpectedly, with a figure from the fairly distant past, whose methods are often and understandably criticized
today: Wilhelm Dörpfeld. In several ways, one could argue that
his field methods during his long campaigns of excavation in the
Nidri Plain on the island of Leukas in western Greece (Figure 1)
in the years 1901–13 were anything but exemplary. These excavations are chiefly remembered for the motive that inspired
them: Dörpfeld's unshakable conviction, in the face of powerful
counterarguments and at the cost of disparagement, even ridi-
cule, from contemporaries, that Leukas, rather than the island
more recently called Ithaka, was to be identified with the Ithaka
of the Homeric *Odyssey*. This conviction was not by any means
an absurd one; it has not been conclusively disproved in the sub-

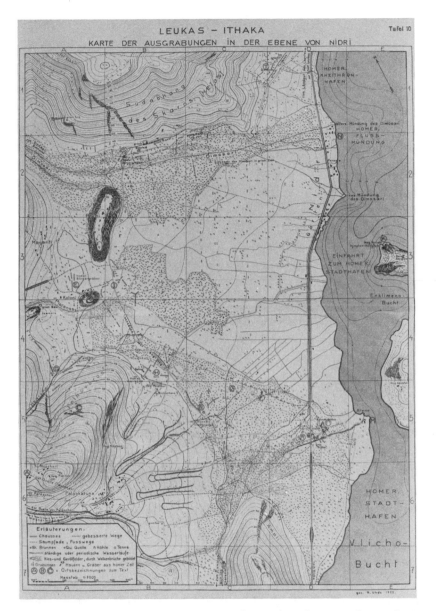

Figure 1. Dörpfeld's excavations in the Nidri Plain, Leukas (plan)
(after W. Dörpfeld).

sequent eighty years, and as late as 1949 the first edition of the
Oxford Classical Dictionary held that the question "remains an
open one." Dörpfeld was insistent, at least when he thought carefully about what he was saying, that the purpose of his excavations on Leukas was not to *prove* the identity of Leukas and Homeric Ithaka, but to *test* the general validity of his theories.[16] He
thus displayed a realistic grasp of the fact that no archaeological
find from a prehistoric era can, in principle, *demonstrate* the
identification of an entity such as "the palace of Odysseus." He
had witnessed at first hand the skepticism that, in some quarters,
had greeted even the general import of Schliemann's discoveries
at Hissarlik, Mycenae, and Tiryns. By this criterion, his excavations were far from being the fiasco that some opponents suggested; we can take him at his word when he says that he was
very satisfied with their results. As later knowledge showed,
these results did not serve his ulterior purpose well, since they
were mostly not of the appropriate date for the setting of the *Odyssey*. Yet what he found and the way he found it were both in
themselves rather impressive, especially for the first decade of this
century.

His preliminary travels on Leukas, besides persuading him of
its identity as Homer's Ithaka, led him to one locality, the Nidri
Plain (Figure 2), as being the main focus of prehistoric settlement
on the island. Various considerations deriving from the text of
the *Odyssey* disposed him to look for a town and a palace not
centered on a hilltop citadel, like Mycenae or Troy, but located
on level ground. He predicted that he would find them in the Ni-

16. Most clearly, in his controversy with Wilamowitz: "Da ich mehrmals
ausdrücklich erklärt habe, daß ich durch diese Grabungen nicht erst die Iden-
tität von Leukas mit dem homerischen Ithaka beweisen will, sondern nur die
Probe auf die Richtigkeit meiner Darlegungen zu machen gedenke, so ist mir
Sinn und Ton seiner [i.e., Wilamowitz's] Worte nicht verständlich. Ich habe al-
len Grund, mit den bisherigen Resultaten der Grabungen zufrieden zu sein"
(*AA* [1904], 74). But elsewhere, notably in *Alt-Ithaka* (Berlin, 1927), 120, 150,
154, he states candidly that the goal of the excavations in the Nidri Plain was
to find "die Stadt des Odysseus."

Figure 2. General view of the Nidri Plain.

dri Plain and trusted his arguments enough to commit himself, year after year, to covering this considerable area with search trenches. They were deep trenches (Figure 3): on average, he reached prehistoric levels only four to six meters down. (A first point of interest is indeed the fact that the prehistoric land surfaces, correctly and observantly identified by him from the scatters of potsherds, had been so deeply buried under later alluvial deposits: Dörpfeld's experience at Olympia, one of the few major Greek sites where a similar state of affairs prevailed, must have helped him here.) The search trenches—which appear in Figure 1 as straggling lines of oblong symbols, mostly running north-south across the plain—were for a long time unsuccessful in locating anything in the form of architectural traces. But Dörpfeld was generations ahead of his time in recognizing and seeing the significance of buried prehistoric land surfaces, frustrated though he undoubtedly was by the absence of actual buildings.

Eventually, his luck changed. Every one of the lettered symbols in Figure 1 represents a significant discovery of these years, and

Figure 3. View of one of Dörpfeld's trenches, Nidri Plain, Leukas.

we shall concentrate on half a dozen of them. The map is laid out in 500-meter squares, and we can see from the density of these major finds that Dörpfeld had not been following a will-o'-the-wisp. His eye for a major locus of prehistoric settlement—surely *the* major locus on the island, as the nature of the finds will confirm—had not failed him. Besides many scattered graves, he found three major prehistoric burial grounds: a huge Early Bronze Age one, with at least thirty-three circles of graves, at *R* (towards the bottom right of Figure 1), and two large Middle Bronze Age ones at *F* (northwest of *R*) and *S* (towards the top left). He found a settlement of oval houses—probably Middle Bronze Age—on the slopes of the hill Amali above the plain (bottom, right of center, not marked with a letter). He found a system of water pipes (line of alternate dashes and dots, running northeastwards to *B*, lower center), which he also claimed as prehistoric. And he found a massive building, whose side wall ran for forty meters, at *P* (close to *R*), which he naturally identified as a palace, though once again it is most probably of Early Bronze Age date: the foundations lay below the water table, which helps to explain why, to this day, the building remains incompletely excavated.[17]

Dörpfeld seldom seems to have laid aside his *Odyssey* text; yet, consciously or otherwise, he was operating, not as an unsuccessful exponent of Homeric studies, but as a first-class field archaeologist. The truly significant thing about his discoveries is that, irrespective of his original hypothesis, they remain, eighty years later, the richest and most informative finds of their period that have been made anywhere in the western half of the Greek homeland, partly thanks to the fact that Dörpfeld published them all in commendable detail. The *R* graves are arguably the

17. For the *R* graves, see *Alt-Ithaka* (cited above, n. 16), 178, 181, 184–86, 217–50; *F* graves, 173, 213–17; *S* graves, 164, 179, 181, 207–13; settlement on Amali hill, 175, 201–3; water system, 159, 196–98; large building, 174–75, 177–78, 198–201.

most impressive of their period from anywhere in Greece, and their contents imply that they are a guide to the location of the leading settlement on Leukas, and perhaps in a wider area of western Greece. None of this would have been achieved had his actual operational methods not been so sound, so exhaustive, and (for 1901) so pioneering.

Different archaeologists will draw different morals from this story. For some, it will exemplify classical archaeology's subservience to literary aims. But this reasonable criticism of the subject as a whole must not be allowed to shade off into the untenable claim that it is thereby prevented from practicing "good," or alternatively "real," archaeology. Dörpfeld's discoveries are none the less real, or his methods (for their day) less good, because of his application, or misapplication, of the principle that an archaeological reality could be searched for behind the Homeric epics. The principle itself, in its general outlines, can hardly be disparaged without qualification, after the extraordinary archaeological results that it yielded between the years 1870 and 1940.

I shall develop the case by two further examples taken, unlike Dörpfeld's, from the central historical periods that are the strict concern of classical archaeology, and taken also from more recent practice. First, Olympia, where in the 1870s German excavators had conducted an inconclusive search for a building described 1,700 years earlier in Pausanias's *Description of Greece* (5.15.1): the workshop in which, six centuries earlier still, the sculptor Pheidias had worked on his statue of Zeus, which became one of the Seven Wonders of the ancient world. The general location, west of the main sanctuary, was not in doubt and two buildings, A and C, had emerged as the likely candidates, without the evidence making a choice between them possible. In 1954, under Emil Kunze, the Germans returned to the search (Figure 4): they were looking for the traces of sculptural activity that had eluded their predecessors, and for evidence that would date that

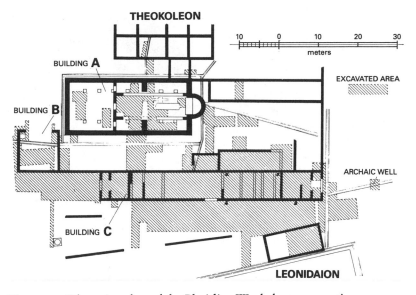

Figure 4. Olympia: plan of the Pheidias Workshop excavations, 1954–58 (after A. Mallwitz).

activity.[18] Outside the south wall of "Building *A*," and partly underlying (and therefore predating) "Building *C*," they found both in ample quantity. This enabled them to identify "Building *A*" (so far as I know, to unanimous acceptance) as the workshop of Pheidias. It also enabled them to settle—to general if not quite universal satisfaction—a controversy over the dating of the statue within Pheidias's career, even though the differing views in that controversy spanned, at most, a period of only thirty years. It threw direct and detailed light, for the first time, on Greek

18. For the excavation in general, see A. Mallwitz and W. Schiering, *Die Werkstatt des Pheidias in Olympia*, vol. 1, Olympische Forschungen, no. 5 (Berlin, 1964); but the fullest account of the sculptural material remains that of E. Kunze in *Neue Deutsche Ausgrabungen im Mittelmeergebiet und im Vorderen Orient* (Berlin, 1959), 277–95. On the problems of interpretation of the molds, see H.-V. Herrmann, *Olympia: Heiligtum und Wettkampfstätte* (Munich, 1972), 254 n. 605; further study is being undertaken by W. Schiering.

Figure 5. Two views of the mug inscribed with Pheidias's name.

methods of workmanship in the untypical materials (gold, ivory, wood, and other substances) in which this and other exceptional statues are known to have been made. But it also included a more spectacular find: a black-glazed mug, on the underside of whose foot are scratched the words "I belong to Pheidias" (Figure 5). The amusing, but unworthy, rumor arising from the feeling that this find was "too good to be true"—that the inscription was a hoax, perhaps by a mischievous, if gifted, student—has now, it seems, been laid to rest: microscopic examination of the surface of the clay within the actual area of the incised letters has shown that the incision was done long ago, and before the diagonal break (itself of considerable age) occurred (Figure 6).[19]

Here, then, was an excavation designed to solve one, and if possible two, problems, and that solved them both: one at least (that of location) not merely with a reasonable degree of plausibility, but beyond any reasonable doubt. This conclusion must stand, I think, even though later research suggests that the position with the sculptural material is more complicated than was first apparent: not *all* of it may in fact be associated with Phei-

19. See W.-D. Heilmeyer, "Antike Werkstättenfunde in Griechenland," *AA* (1981), 447–48.

Figure 6. Close-up view of the Pheidias inscription.

dias's work on his colossal statue, and the workshop may have been used again later. As we have seen, however, Pheidias's activity here is beyond question.

My final example involves another great work of classical antiquity: the combined sundial and calendar erected by the emperor Augustus in the Campus Martius at Rome in 9 B.C. In 1976 by means of a complex series of arguments, mathematical, astronomical, and archaeological, Edmund Buchner reached certain conclusions about the location, level, form, and function of the gigantic horizontal network, some 160 by 75 meters in area, where the readings of the sundial were taken (Figure 7). He was working largely from a single archaeological datum: the known location and approximate height of the obelisk that had formed the pointer of the sundial, which had been found in 1748, but reerected on a different site. He ended his argument with the words: "A mere fragment of this network would afford us a picture of the whole—and confirm or refute my conclusions,"[20] cou-

20. "Schon ein Stückchen des Liniennetzes könnte uns ein Bild vom ganzen vermitteln—und meine Ergebnisse bestätigen oder widerlegen" ("Solarium Augusti und Ara Pacis," *RM* 83 [1976]: 365; the article was reprinted in E. Buchner, *Die Sonnenuhr des Augustus* [Mainz, 1982]).

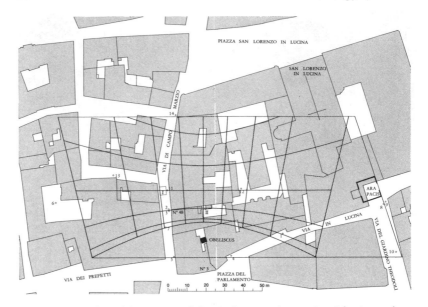

Figure 7. Deduced location of the *Solarium Augusti*, with sites of excavations of 1979 and 1980 (after E. Buchner).

pling this with a prediction that, on grounds of the known later history of the site, the evidence of the network would be there to find.

Three years later he set out to test these conclusions by excavation: and that in a heavily built-up area near the heart of the modern city, where the very largest available space (Figure 8) would be afforded by the width of a narrow street. It was in fact in the cellar of a house (48 Via di Campo Marzio), where Buchner had predicted the intersection of two "month-spaces" in the calendar portion of the network, that the decisive find occurred. Here, at a depth of well over six meters below street level, was found a travertine block into which a nine-inch-high, bronze letter *A* had been embedded in lead. Other letters soon followed, showing that the *A* was the second letter of PARTHENOS—Virgo in the more familiar Latin form of the zodiacal calendar (Figure 9). In this case, as with Kunze's find at Olympia, the full picture

Figure 8. *Solarium Augusti*: view of 1979 excavation in the Via di Campo Marzio.

Figure 9. *Solarium Augusti*: view of 1980 excavation in the cellar of no. 48, Via di Campo Marzio.

once again turned out to be slightly less clear-cut than first impressions had suggested. Buchner struck the sundial network at a slightly higher level than predicted, and the reason later became plain: this was not Augustus's original sundial, but a slightly later (perhaps Domitianic) replacement, which for obvious reasons had to be located exactly on top of its predecessor (since the obelisk presumably had not then been moved).[21] But again, as at Olympia, the location and identification had been established beyond any doubt.

What do these instances, collectively or individually, prove? What strengths of classical archaeology do they illustrate? At the simplest level, they show excavators testing hypotheses and validating their general soundness—in the latter two cases proving their specific correctness. This last is pretty rare in real-life archaeology. Where else but in the classical world can one dig a narrow hole twenty-one feet deep and find at the bottom almost exactly what one predicted? Where else could you excavate the site of a known individual's activity 2,400 years earlier and find the actual autograph of that individual? I am aware that similar things do occasionally happen in the archaeology of Egypt, of the Near East, and of China; and one might add that they happen all the time in that other archaeology, the one that the layman encounters most often—archaeology as depicted by the mass media. *Raiders of the Lost Ark* is only one of the more recent in a long line of variations on this theme. But all this is far from the normal experience of any archaeologist, and apparently even further from the ideals of the new archaeology. Yet how great, in reality, is this last-mentioned distance, and in what exactly does it consist?

In many ways, the most impressive feature of these three instances is what took place before excavation began. Dörpfeld ex-

21. See E. Buchner, "Horologium Solarium Augusti," *RM* 87 (1980): 355–73, likewise reprinted in *Die Sonnenuhr des Augustus* (cited above, n. 20).

amined the landscape of a sizeable piece of territory and then committed himself to one smaller part of it as being the likeliest location of what he was looking for. Though not in the way he had hoped, his judgment was vindicated in a way that has been perhaps of at least equal benefit to archaeology at large. Kunze set out to find the solution to two controversies, each at least eighty years old, and did so convincingly. Buchner developed a complex and highly specific hypothesis and committed himself to it in print before testing it with resounding success. Thus far, these excavators were observing the precepts of the new archaeology: "Develop explicit assumptions and then test them"; "Cross the boundary lines of disciplines, making outward contributions to the other disciplines if possible"; "Count, measure, and quantify where possible"—all these maxims are exemplified by one or more of the cases illustrated.

But from this point on a gulf begins to open up. Three of the strongest pejorative terms used by the new archaeologists to condemn traditional approaches are "blind empiricism," "pure description," and "particularism." Now I hope to have shown that by no stretch of imagination can the first of these charges be made to stick here: the methods of the three excavators were anything but "blindly empirical."

As for the second charge, I have heard the phrase "purely descriptive" applied to the whole discipline of classical archaeology, most often in contrast with "explanatory" or "explicatory," used of approaches directed at answering the question "Why?" It might be argued that each of these discoveries opened up questions of an explanatory kind, about which the excavators themselves probably pondered. In Dörpfeld's case, the obvious question was why a Greek place-name, "Ithaka," should have migrated from one island to another between the time of the formation of the Homeric epic and the dawn of Greek history, as on his view it would have to have done; and we know that he was much exercised by this problem. Kunze's finds showed, as most would agree, that the statue of Zeus at Olympia was the work of

Pheidias's old age, after his great commission in the Parthenon at Athens. But in that case how and why did a strong ancient tradition grow up that he was prosecuted and died in prison in the immediate aftermath of his work in Athens? Buchner's discovery of the early replacement of Augustus's sundial suggests a connection with the fact (attested by Pliny the Elder a few years after its construction) that the original sundial began to go progressively wrong in its time-keeping. Why did this happen? Yet, when all is said, we must admit that the actual fieldwork I have described was not in *itself* directed at answering these questions.

It has similarly to be conceded that these achievements also fall foul of the third criticism: they are decidedly particularistic. And, in Lewis Binford's words, "Once . . . the focus of study moves to comparative pattern recognition and evaluation of variability, particularistic approaches are thereafter trivial, uninteresting and boring even to their advocates."[22] With the last four words, Binford unquestionably goes too far—we have seen how and why particular approaches continue to interest some of us—but let that pass. More important is the fact that some new archaeologists have conceded that particularistic approaches can act as a springboard for other advances of a more approved kind. Thus, in the very book in whose introduction Binford uses the words just quoted, Stanley South writes: "The fact that Noël Hume uses the particularistic approach does not mean that the descriptive classifications and data emerging from his work cannot be used for other approaches."[23] I would go further and say that, without both the foundation and the contrast provided by traditional work carried out in the "particularistic" spirit, the new archaeologists would find it very much harder to make headway with the theoretical, universalizing, anthropologically oriented, and, at times, law-seeking approaches they pursue. It is hard to imagine a better springboard than Dörpfeld's (at least for

22. Introduction to S. South, *Method and Theory* (cited above, n. 14), xi.
23. *Method and Theory*, 10.

its period) for further work on prehistoric settlement and land use in the area in question; or than Kunze's for that most exotic manifestation of human creative enterprise, sculpture in gold and ivory; or than Buchner's for the study of early time measurement. We have seen classical archaeology excelling just where we should expect it to excel: in finding a right, or at least an exceedingly convincing, answer to questions that have a single answer.

Archaeology needs *both* approaches. It needs to confirm its theoretical hypotheses, not once, but repeatedly, and if some of the confirmations approach total certainty, as is only possible in a field such as classical archaeology, with its outstandingly rich data base, then archaeology will be the better for it. In classical archaeology, I admit, it is the generalizing approach that is in short supply, but I do not think that it matters very much whether this lack is made good by insiders or outsiders. If the insiders were by some means to achieve this, however, it would be reassuring to be able to feel that the fact would at least be noticed by other archaeologists.

"History is, strictly speaking, the study of questions; the study of answers belongs to anthropology and sociology. . . . Culture is history which has become dormant or extinct," W. H Auden asserted.[24] Most archaeology deals with time-spans of such length that it inevitably concerns itself with "culture" to the same degree anthropology does. Most, but not quite all. There are epochs in man's past where the state of the evidence is such that it allows archaeologists to study "questions" that were then, often for the first time, being asked; and to examine the material evidence for the first attempts to answer them, rather than the "extinct history" of the widely accepted answer. Classical archaeology deals with perhaps the most important of these exceptional epochs. Yet not everything in classical archaeology falls into this class of enquiry, and history itself studies many different kinds of

24. *The Dyer's Hand*, Vintage Books edition (New York, 1968), 97.

questions. I shall attempt in subsequent chapters to show how the subject could increase its intellectual vitality by stepping over some of the artificial boundaries, narrower than those the restrictions of the discipline themselves impose, that it has allowed itself to accept.

CHAPTER TWO

Archaeology and History

Between the first edition, in 1949, of the *Oxford Classical Dictionary* and the second in 1970, it was evidently thought desirable completely to rewrite the entry for "Archaeology (Classical)." One of the changes John Cook, in the later version, made from Stanley Casson's earlier entry was to omit, without replacing it by any obvious substitute, a statement about classical archaeology that read as follows: "Its contributions to the study of ancient history are direct and obvious." Deliberate or otherwise, the omission of this sentence is so precisely in harmony with my argument that I should like to take it as a text, or rather non-text, for this chapter.

If it is generally agreed that the main strand of activity in traditional classical archaeology has been, as stated at the outset, the study of ancient works of art, then it will probably also be accepted that the next most prominent strand has been its interaction with ancient history. It is the former field that has provided the greatest names in the history of the subject, and in which its prestige accordingly stands highest not only with other classicists, who can find in this activity qualities that they appreciate—some utility, a kind of analogy for their own work, and (always important for them) criteria by which to judge excellence—but also perhaps with the public at large, which, insofar as it is aware of classical archaeology at all, probably sees this as its main function. Nevertheless, I wish to postpone consideration of this aspect until a later chapter. I do so, not because I think that classical archaeology is invulnerable to criticism on this front; nor yet for a second reason, that this whole field of activity is anathema to the school of thought represented by the new archaeology, though that is beyond all question the case. Rather, it is because I feel that the most urgent need for change may lie in the second sphere, and more specifically in the interrelation of Greek archaeology with Greek history.

The rapprochement between these two subjects is time-honored and used to be accepted with little question—as is implied by the earlier version of the *Oxford Classical Dictionary* entry—by both sides. As a result, it has become close: closer, perhaps, than in any other field of ancient studies where a parallel partnership of archaeology and history is possible, with the single exception of the much more stormy marriage between Old Testament history and archaeology in modern Israel. But like other outwardly harmonious relationships, it may owe some of its peacefulness to the tacit, but firm, assumption that one of the two parties is subordinate. This is suggested by the description of archaeology, evidently current in classical circles a couple of generations ago, as "the handmaid of history."[1] I shall not waste time in protest at this image, but instead argue that Greek archaeology, at any rate, has been married to, or waiting on, the wrong kind of history.

This needs first elucidation and then exemplification. My thesis here is part of a wider claim already made elsewhere: that classical archaeology, a subject dominated for some time past by various kinds of positivism, has in the process succumbed to a form

1. This perhaps now obsolete dictum is cited by T. J. Dunbabin, *The Greeks and Their Eastern Neighbours* (London, 1957), 14.

of "positivist fallacy."[2] The fallacy consists in making archaeological prominence and historical importance into almost inter-
changeable terms: in equating what is observable with what is
significant. It can be exemplified in many an interpretation of an
excavated settlement site. The line of argument is apt to run
along some such lines as the following: "In the sequence of deposits on our site, this, this, and this are the most prominent features" (referring often to architectural changes, including the destruction of buildings, but also to such features as a change in the
incidence of high-quality or imported goods). "Therefore, the episodes these features represent were the most important episodes
in the history of the site. Therefore it is right to consult the documentary records for the classical world at this time, to see which
recorded events could be represented, or exemplified, by these
features on our site." I believe that each of the steps in such an
argument is most likely to be mistaken.

But first, let us try to approach the issue from the historical
side. The subject matter of Greek history used traditionally to
consist of the study of the great political, constitutional, and military episodes that seem to have had a decisive effect on the development of Greek civilization. In recent years, activity has been
extended to cover the great "constants"—slavery, demography,
popular morality, relations between the sexes, agriculture, animal husbandry, and death and burial—just as has happened in
medieval and modern history. But the formative years of classical
archaeology as a discipline coincided with the "old order" of history (as, indeed, of art history), and it has been slower than they
in responding to changes of course. In part, this may be because
it was receiving the signals at second hand; but in part, also, because it appeared to be doing rather a useful job as things were.

Many important politico-military episodes of the sixth, fifth,
fourth, third, and second centuries B.C. in Greece can be dated to

2. In M. H. Crawford, ed., *Sources for Ancient History* (Cambridge,
1983), 137–84, especially 142–43, 145–46, 163.

the year, and some to the month or day. Since many kinds of Greek material artifact (it should be noted that I am excluding coins and inscriptions from the definition of archaeology) are held to be dateable to within twenty-five years or less, it would seem a reasonable inference that the results of a carefully observed excavation can be brought to bear on traditional history. This process can be expected to take one of three main forms: that of confirming or accentuating existing historical knowledge; that of supplementing it; and that of contradicting and potentially negating it. In the central epochs of Greek history—central, that is, both chronologically and geographically—the confirming function is expected to be the norm. The further one moves away from the geographical center of the central and southern Greek mainland or from the chronological center of the fifth and fourth centuries B.C. (and in the case of Greece this means primarily moving to *earlier* periods), the scantier and less reliable the historical documentation is likely to be, and the greater the scope for the supplementary or the contradictory roles for the archaeological evidence. A comparable process applies in Roman history as one moves away from Italy to the provinces and from the central epoch of the late Republic and early Empire—in this case especially when moving to *later* periods. In the earlier history of Greece, several episodes spring to mind as involving at least as much archaeological as historical evidence in any modern discussion of them: colonization, the rise of the *polis*, the "Lelantine War," the adoption of the armor and tactics of the hoplite, the beginning of the building of oared warships, not to mention more obviously archaeological topics such as the appearance of monumental architecture. I wish to take a closer look presently at the first subject on this list; but first we need to consider again the alleged "positivist fallacy," and one specific kind of proposition to which it gives rise.

Starting from the hypothetical line of reasoning sketched above, many excavators of classical sites set out to express their results in essentially the form of traditional historical narrative: to conclude, that is, that given events involving their sites took place at given approximate dates. The practice is equally accepted, if only as a kind of convenient shorthand, by both archaeologists and historians. But it is open to two lines of critical examination. One is narrow, technical, and of only "particularistic" interest—the chronological one. How has the dating of the archaeological material been established within the desired margin of precision? Is it *entirely* free of dependence on the date of the presumed historical event with which it is here being associated, or is there any taint of circularity about the argument? And in any case, are we sure that it is sound? The other line of enquiry is more abstract and far-reaching: it refers not to the accuracy of the given approximate dates, but to the reality of the given events.

Let us return to reexamine the exact nature of the hypothetical excavator's argument, summarized above. If he is really identifying features or episodes on his site with known historical events, then he must be stating (or assuming) the following steps of argument: first, the conclusion *that* a given episode took place; then, an inference as to approximately *when* it took place; finally, an inference as to roughly *how* it took place—that is, in what circumstances, not necessarily yet from what causes. The next phase in the argument, identification with a known historical event, will in most cases provide the causation. Thus an equation is made between a direct and recent observation in the soil and a preexisting historical datum, usually in the form of an assertion by an ancient writer that may be in some degree an abstraction or interpretation of events, rather than a plain factual statement.

Everyone will probably agree that, in *relative* terms, the successive steps in this argument—the "that," the "when," the "how," and the equation with the historical event—represent a sequence of ascending controversiality. What I shall be arguing is that from the very first step, the assertion that the archaeological episode is "present," the whole sequence is enveloped in greater doubt than anyone seems ready to admit, in public at least. Here I can draw on a not unexpected ally from within the new archaeology. I understand from his former pupils that David Clarke used to enlarge on this very point in his teaching; and he published at least one statement of warning: "The danger of historical narrative as a vehicle for archaeological results is that it pleases by virtue of its smooth coverage and apparent finality, whilst the data on which it is based are never comprehensive, never capable of supporting but one interpretation and rest upon complex probabilities. Archaeological data are not historical data and consequently archaeology is not history."[3] The incompleteness, ambiguity, and complexity of archaeological findings are the very qualities that I have in mind here.

First, the incompleteness. If an archaeologist reports that a settlement site that he is excavating was burned and then abandoned, the historian and the layman in general will understand him to mean the settlement as a whole, or at least very substantial parts of it. In fact, of course, such an inference is only secure when the settlement has been entirely, or very largely, excavated. Even in Greece, where some settlements have been under intermittent excavation for over a hundred years, this condition is very seldom satisfied. Even when it is, and a horizon of destruction is found everywhere, the conclusion that this destruction was synchronous, that it was all a single episode, is likely to be based on common sense inference rather than on demonstration: the degree of precision, in even the best-dated pottery series, is unlikely to justify a distinction between one day and, say, ten years. It may be unnecessary to remind ourselves that documented history offers cases of a settlement being destroyed twice within a very short time. Furthermore, destruction deposits frequently (and predictably) contain material that was far from brand-new at the time of the disaster. We see, therefore, that the

3. D. L. Clarke, *Analytical Archaeology* (London, 1968; 2nd ed. 1978, ed. R. Chapman), 12.

factor of incompleteness affects the application of both the "that" and the "when" to such episodes as the destruction of a settlement.

Ambiguity and complexity likewise affect both these matters and, more especially, the question "how?" The distinction between natural disasters, such as earthquake and accidental fire, and the results of military action becomes a crucial one in the context of historical reconstruction. Yet for the archaeologist excavating a site, it is often very obscure, even imperceptible. There is an area of especial doubt centered round the question of how far the military resources of the ancient world were capable of visiting *total* destruction on the whole surface area of a settlement. Even the slaughter of an entire population, followed by permanent abandonment of the site, could easily be encompassed without leaving archaeologically traceable evidence. Let us consider a (to date) unfulfilled hypothesis. We read in the ancient sources (Thucydides 7.29; Pausanias 1.23.3 and 9.19.4) that the Boeotian town of Mykalessos was sacked by rampaging Thracian mercenary troops on the Athenian side in the Peloponnesian War in 413 B.C. They are said to have killed every living thing that they met, and to have pillaged temples and houses. Now the site of Mykalessos has been identified with great probability (see p. 82 below), but the settlement, as opposed to the cemeteries, has yet to be excavated. If and when it is, how apparent will the material traces of the episode of 413 B.C. be? The pottery styles of that date are at a relatively closely dated phase in their sequence. Pausanias, who was writing nearly six hundred years later, implies in the first passage cited above that the disaster was so horrific that Mykalessos was never resettled; and evidently it was indeed abandoned by his day. Yet there is already evidence that, irrespective of the correctness of the modern identification of the site, Pausanias was mistaken; for there are coins of Mykalessos of the fourth century B.C. (and one might add that the burials associated with the presumed site of Mykalessos run from the eighth to the third centuries B.C.). It is not fair to censure future excavators for what they may or may not do; but on the showing of past practice, I am tempted to say that traces of destruction on the site, whether securely dated or not, will all be presumptively associated with the sack of 413 B.C.; and that, if they should not materialize at all, the identification of the site will be called into question (failing conclusive epigraphic evidence), possibly by scholars other than the excavators themselves. Different problems will arise if the sequence of occupation does not match the evidence of the coinage, and of the nearby graves. And so on.

But a clearer illustration of the areas of incompleteness, ambiguity, and complexity in archaeological evidence is offered, not once but many times over, by the experience of Aegean Late Bronze Age archaeology—perhaps the first field that springs to mind when the interpretation of settlement destructions is mentioned. It would not be fair to dwell on the chronological aspect too much, since everyone would agree that the dating of the sequences of pottery and other artifacts is less precise than in fully historical periods. But there have been some striking examples of uncertainty as to whether major Bronze Age sites have suffered military destruction, and, if so, when and how. It will suffice to mention three instances, and dwell at slightly greater length on a fourth.

First, the now long-standing debate about the destruction of palatial Knossos. The past twenty-five years have witnessed a movement, of gradually accumulating force, towards lowering Sir Arthur Evans's original date of about 1400 B.C. for this episode, not to mention a number of variant surmises about its cause. Many now favor a destruction date as late as c. 1200 B.C.; intermediate positions are, however, also held, including the one that there were *two* levels of destruction, one not very long after

1400 and one close to 1200 B.C.[4] Next, the somewhat younger, but in some ways similar, debate about the destruction of the Mycenaean palace at Thebes: here again, there has been strong recent pressure for lowering the date advanced by the original excavator, A. D. Keramopoullos; and here again it is a reputable view that there were two destructions rather than one.[5] One of the common features underlying these two cases is also present in a third, involving not the destruction but the mere abandonment of a site, Tell-el-Amarna in Egypt.[6] All these instances exemplify an archaeological technicality that is seldom communicated to the layman. The repeated tendency towards the lowering of an archaeological date for the *end* of a period of occupation is not entirely a matter of coincidence. It usually arises from the later extension of knowledge. The resumption of excavation within a site often reveals fresh pottery deposits in a destruction context: when these deposits are earlier than those previously known, the find may attract little attention, since a deposit must be dated by the latest material in it; but when the new finds are *later*—and, by the law of averages, this can be predicted to happen sometimes—then this must result in adjustment. Alternatively, it is not further excavation, but further study of the material already known, or of its precise excavation context, that leads to the same result. Roughly speaking, the former process is what has taken place with Thebes, and the latter with Knossos and Tell-el-Amarna. The adjustment may be made in "historical" terms ("Palatial Knossos and Thebes were destroyed close to 1200, rather than close to 1400 B.C.") or, if the historical chro-

4. For a full and recent summary of this debate, see W.-D. Niemeier, "Mycenaean Knossos and the Age of Linear B," *SMEA* 23 (1982): 219–87.

5. H. W. Catling, J. F. Cherry, R. E. Jones, and J. T. Killen survey the Thebes debate in "The Linear B Inscribed Stirrup Jars and West Crete," *BSA* 75 (1980): 49–113, especially 94–98.

6. See V. Hankey, "The Aegean Deposit at El Amarna," in *Acts of the International Archaeological Symposium "The Mycenaeans in the Eastern Mediterranean"* (Nicosia, 1973), 126–36.

nology is too well established to be moved, then it is the purely archaeological time-scale that has to be shifted ("When Tell-el-Amarna was abandoned rather before 1350 B.C., the pottery style called Late Helladic III A, rather than being in mid career, was already over"). All these three instances are important enough to have an effect on the "historical" reconstruction of the Aegean Late Bronze Age, and to have already led to the embarrassed rewriting of narrative accounts. All should serve as dire warnings to the historian of later periods who seeks to derive historical narrative from archaeological observation.

Even more critical, however, is the case of Mycenae, involving as it does the fate of many of the other major sites that shared in the same culture. It is widely held that three successive horizons of destruction are detectable at Mycenae itself, and that the second of these is of the greatest historical moment, since it can be equated with the main episode of destruction at Tiryns, Pylos, and other sites. The first destruction at Mycenae is largely or entirely confined to buildings outside the citadel itself, and belongs to a late, perhaps very late, stage in the lifetime of the "Late Helladic IIIB" phase of Mycenaean pottery. The second destruction belongs at the end of this same phase, and affects most structures within the citadel. We shall turn in a moment to the third destruction.

The line that divides the first two destructions is, in strict ceramic terms, a fine one: it is reasonable to ask whether knowledge of the Mycenaean pottery sequence has yet reached the point where a clear and incontrovertible distinction can be maintained between stages "towards the end of" and "at the end of" a given phase. The same doubts reassert themselves when the equation is made with the sequence on other sites at some distance from Mycenae. There may have been a further element, hidden though perfectly respectable, in the reasoning in respect of Mycenae itself: that common sense would lead us to expect outlying and undefended buildings to "fall" earlier than strongly fortified ones. But what gives the matter added interest is the view, convincingly advanced by one of the most recent excavators of Mycenae in 1975, that the first horizon of destruction at Mycenae was, in any case, partly or entirely brought about by earthquake, and not by the military action that was tacitly assumed in most earlier reconstructions.[7] Not only that, but a resumption of the German excavations at Tiryns, only a few miles away to the south, has now yielded equally convincing evidence of destruction by earthquake there; but in this case, the disaster is that of the *final*, or "great" destruction, affecting the palace and citadel. The director of these excavations, K. Kilian, has drawn the natural conclusion that what holds for Tiryns must also hold for Mycenae: at both sites, the second and decisive horizon of disaster was also brought about by earthquake.[8] Thus two successive "military episodes" at Mycenae have to be reinterpreted as natural disasters (if indeed they do not prove to be aspects of one and the same catastrophe), and a whole series of attempts to account for the fall of Mycenaean civilization are thereby largely vitiated.

There remains, however, the third and final "destruction" at Mycenae. In 1924 A. J. B. Wace published the results of his excavation of a building lying just inside the citadel walls that he identified as a granary.[9] He found it to have been burned at a date considerably later than that of the main catastrophe in the citadel—that is, some way into the ensuing Late Helladic IIIC period—though he did not claim that this episode was part of a wide horizon of destruction at Mycenae. But this single datum of archaeological observation, a fire that could not be shown to have affected more than one modest-sized building, became a

7. G. E. Mylonas, most recently in *Mycenae Rich in Gold* (Athens, 1983), 145–48, 161.

8. See K. Kilian, "Zum Ende der Mykenischen Epoche in der Argolis," *Jahrb. RGZM* 27 (1980): 166–95, especially 182, 185 with fig. 7.

9. "Excavations at Mycenae: The Granary," *BSA* 25 (1921–23): 38–61.

kind of symbol: the "granary destruction" at Mycenae was for a long time the most positive material trace that approximately corresponded in time to the indications, given by several ancient writers, of the date of the onslaught of the Dorians in the Peloponnese (that is, the later part of the twelfth century B.C. in our terms). Few heeded the sensible opinion, advanced in 1962 by the Swedish scholar Per Ålin, that the destruction of the granary at Mycenae was most probably the result of an accidental fire. Here again, later work at Tiryns has produced a corresponding level of destruction in at least one house within the citadel; but this observation loses any dramatic quality that it may possess once one learns that the selfsame house suffered no less than three destructions by fire within a single subphase of the Late Helladic IIIC period.[10] One can appreciate the natural yearning on the part of layman and scholar alike for a historical reconstruction of some kind, but it can be a disillusioning experience to scrutinize the foundations of those that are offered.

It may be felt, however, that the subject of the Aegean Bronze Age is not "fair game": that its archaeological record is universally recognized to be problematic, and that narrative accounts of it do not seriously claim to be "history." So let us turn, somewhat abruptly, to what might be called the opposite extreme— that is, to a relatively well documented period over a millennium later. I hope to show that here, too, very similar conditions prevail and almost equally intractable problems present themselves. The place and time that I have in mind are the confines of the Roman Empire in the second century A.D. In the prolonged attempts of the Roman armies to establish a firm northern frontier for the province of Britannia, a striking, though relatively brief,

10. P. Ålin, *Das Ende der Mykenischen Fundstätten auf dem griechischen Festland*, Studies in Mediterranean Archaeology, no. 1 (Lund, 1962), 150; cf. 12–13, 15, 24. For contemporary destruction at Tiryns, see Kilian (cited above, n. 8), 183–86, fig. 7, supplemented by later reports in *AA* (1981), 159; (1982), 395–96; (1983), 280–81.

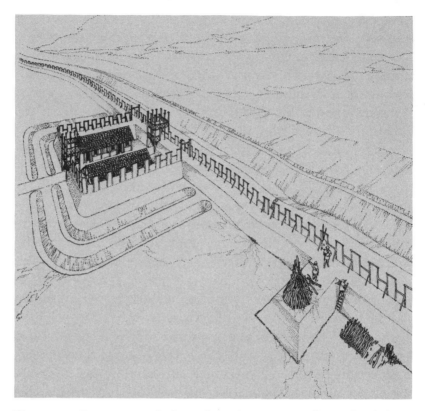

Figure 10. Reconstructed view of the Antonine Wall, Scotland, from the east (after D. J. Breeze).

episode was the building of the Antonine Wall in lowland Scotland (Figure 10). Here it is agreed by all parties, including such ancient historical sources as there are, that in or about A.D. 142 the emperor Antoninus Pius commissioned the building of a barrier across the isthmus between the estuaries of the Forth and the Clyde, the narrowest point on the whole mainland of Great Britain. It is further agreed—though this time no ancient source directly attests the point—that excavation shows this Antonine Wall to have been occupied by the Romans for a period, briefly abandoned with some evidence of local destruction, then once more occupied after a certain amount of necessary rebuilding. At this point in the story, archaeological opinion in general agrees that we are still within the principate of Antoninus: that is, that the reoccupation began before his death in A.D. 161. But the story is not yet complete: we have yet to see when the Antonine Wall was finally abandoned by the Romans.

On this question, I cannot do better than quote the words of one of the most recent authorities: "Over the last 100 years the suggested dates have ranged from the 160's through the 180's to 197 and 207 and finally back to the 160's. There is no guarantee that the date of about 163, which is the one now accepted by most scholars, is correct; it is merely the most probable in the light of the evidence available at the present time."[11] Let us first note the combination, in this history of variant dates, of a search for precision on the one hand and subsequent vacillation on the other: the former feature, exemplified by proposals such as "197" and "207," is a sure sign of the attempt to equate archaeological observation with historical event. But what accounts for the relatively wide time-span bracketed by the rival suggestions? This is after all an epoch that, if not the most fully documented in classical history, is very clear in its general outlines: on the historical side, we know many of the regnal dates of the emperors to the month, if not the day, a fact that has immediate repercussions for such finds as coins and inscriptions, which often bear an emperor's name; on the purely archaeological side, too, the primary chronological basis, the pottery series of the workshops of eastern and central Gaul, is relatively accurate. Yet, as we have seen, estimates as to the length of the period of reoccupation have ranged from two years to forty-six years after the death of Antoninus, which forms the latest generally accepted historical terminus.

11. D. J. Breeze, *The Northern Frontiers of Roman Britain* (London, 1982), 118.

Just as much as in the instances from the Aegean Bronze Age, the true explanation, I believe, emerges from the inherent and un-changing features of archaeological excavation, and of the ob-servations derivable from it. We should remind ourselves yet again of the provisional and ambiguous nature of every interpre-tation of such evidence. For one thing, revisions and refinements can take place in the dating of the most copious class of material, the pottery, even though it be within narrower limits than in a prehistoric era.[12] More important, however, are the difficulties in interpreting a stratified sequence of occupations. D. J. Breeze, whose summary of the question I quoted above (n. 11), refers in passing to some of these complexities. There is a recurrent one that derives from the practices of Roman armies: at Birrens (a fort lying behind the Antonine Wall), Breeze notes, "The Roman army may have destroyed the fort itself, preparatory to a change in garrison: such a practice was quite usual"; and at least one fort on the Wall, at New Kilpatrick (Bearsden), seems to have been subjected to this treatment. He also affirms a general point dis-cussed earlier: "While archaeology can prove that a fort was re-built, abandoned for a time or even destroyed, it can rarely prove the reason for such an event."[13]

We must note, too, that the acceptance of the "early" date (c. A.D. 163) for the Roman withdrawal depends on overcoming some awkward pieces of counterevidence: for instance, at one of the Wall forts, Castlecary, a Roman temple was constructed ap-parently well after that date, probably in the 170s or 180s, which must suggest at least a local reoccupation of outposts. One be-gins to see why Sheppard Frere, as recently as 1967, maintained a date in the 180s in his standard textbook on Roman Britain.[14] The issue is further complicated by yet another question: was there or was there not a *third* brief Roman occupation of the

12. On the pottery, see B. R. Hartley, "The Roman Occupations of Scot-land: The Evidence of the Samian Ware," *Britannia* 3 (1972): 1–55.
13. Breeze, *Northern Frontiers* (cited above, n. 11), 120.
14. S. S. Frere, *Britannia* (London, 1967), 155–65.

Wall, after the abandonment that we have been discussing? Sir George Macdonald had in 1934 proposed that there was, but Frere had already found this view "very doubtful," [15] and Breeze seems now to reject it. These uncertainties have arisen notwithstanding the generally high standard of fieldwork on the Antonine Wall, as in Romano-British archaeology in general in recent decades; and despite another important advantage, the relatively small size of the sites, which reduces the risk of misleading results arising from incomplete excavation.

The leap in time and space has not, then, delivered us from the problems and uncertainties that attend archaeological interpretation. On the contrary, this example from a much-studied field of Roman archaeology has proved to exemplify the difficulties involved in each stage of our hypothetical excavator's argument (see p. 38 above). Indeed, the last and most vulnerable step, the equation with historical events, has not been reached, so problematic were the antecedent stages. The possibility of Roman, as well as of enemy, agency in destroying a Roman fort exemplifies the difficulty involved in the question "how?"; evidence like that of the Castlecary temple has obvious bearing on the question "when?"; and even the most elementary step, the inference *that* an episode took place, appears problematic in the case of the "third occupation period."

The main concern of this book is, however, with classical archaeology, and I return to it from these two chastening experiences in adjacent fields. Greek colonization is a topic, and its epoch in general is a period, for which the contribution of archaeology is now recognized as pretty well indispensable. Even as long ago as 1925, when volume 3 of the first edition of the *Cambridge Ancient History* appeared, dealing with the centuries between c. 1000 and 600 B.C., two of the six authors who contributed on early Greece were archaeologists, and a third was J. L. Myres, who, as erstwhile Sather audiences found, had a lot

15. Ibid., 163 and n. 4.

of the archaeologist in him as well. Thus today, when the evidence of dozens of excavated early colonial sites in at least ten modern countries is available, it would be impossible to carry very far a discussion of the nature, dating, and causation of the first Greek colonies without including this material (Figure 11).

It could be maintained that over the past two generations or so, the experience of combining the historical and archaeological evidence in this field has been a reassuring one. The information given by our ancient sources has been at times satisfactorily reinforced, at times usefully supplemented, by the results of excavation. Yet the mere existence of such a consensus is potentially a warning sign that circular arguments have been employed. The vigilant historian, in particular, will want to ask how far the testimony of the excavation finds can stand independently of the historical framework into which they are being fitted. In the case of early Greek colonization in Sicily, the doubts prove to center on the aspect of chronology. Thucydides, in a few precious sentences at the beginning of his sixth book (6.3.1–5.3) offers very specific foundation dates, to the exact year, for a number of the Greek cities in Sicily. At this early period such categorical evidence, even from a source two to three hundred years later in time, is in very short supply; and the early excavators of Syracuse, Gela, and other colonies naturally had Thucydides' dates very much in mind as they searched for the oldest deposits at their sites. More important, the scholars who worked somewhat later to establish an accurate chronology for early Greek pottery styles in general for the first time made more use of these Thucydidean dates than of all other evidence combined.

Let us take the case of the foundation of Gela as an example. Thucydides gives a date, corresponding to the year 689/8 B.C. in our terms, for this event. Fairly extensive early exploration of the site and its cemeteries produced a volume of pottery (much of it, in the opening phases, of Corinthian make), and encouraged the belief that the beginning of this pottery series belonged to the

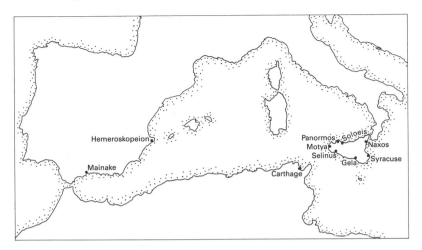

Figure 11. Map showing sites of selected western Greek colonies.

opening years of the colony's life. None of it was earlier than the beginning of the phase called Middle Protocorinthian: it was to be inferred, therefore, that the Middle Protocorinthian style began to be produced around 690 B.C.[16] This line of argument was sound enough, although a little thought will show that it depended on certain "hidden" hypotheses, besides the obvious one of a belief in the correctness of Thucydides' date: for example, the assumption that the presence of a large quantity of Greek pottery implies the presence of Greek settlers, and vice versa.

But how can we set about testing the validity of the argument? Clearly, only evidence discovered *since* the chronological scheme for Corinthian pottery was broadly agreed upon—and that means since Payne published his *Necrocorinthia*[17]—is admissible. The obvious field for further accumulation of evidence lies in continued excavation at Gela. But a little forethought shows

16. This presents the argument in its original form. Later finds have modified the Minor Premiss in much the same way as with Selinus (see below); cf. J. N. Coldstream, *Greek Geometric Pottery* (London, 1968), 326–27.

17. H. G. G. Payne, *Necrocorinthia* (London, 1931), 21–27, an account that built on earlier work by K. Friis Johansen and others.

that such further evidence, while it can only proceed very slowly and laboriously towards the strengthening of the original argument, can very easily and rapidly undermine it. Even the discovery of thousands of further pieces of Middle Protocorinthian at Gela will merely serve to confirm the existing assumption that the lifetime of this style fell within the lifetime of the colony. But by contrast, a single substantial find of *earlier* pottery at Gela will upset the whole argument. We have here roughly the converse of the position with the destruction dates in the Aegean Late Bronze Age: there, the extension of knowledge tended to result in the lowering of dates, but at least the imprecision of the historical data in most cases allowed some space for adjustment. Here, further knowledge can bring about change only in the opposite direction; yet at the same time the presence of a precise historical tradition, in the shape of Thucydides' dates, allows of little or no room for maneuver, and will almost inevitably produce severe tension. At Gela, this process has in fact already begun (see n. 16 above), and in general the difficulty is clearly more serious than in the earlier prehistoric instances. Yet the archaeological realities in the two periods are, I would argue, essentially the same: incompleteness, ambiguity, and complexity are taking their accustomed toll.

A later foundation, Selinus, provides a more substantial illustration. This time, we may try expressing in syllogistic form the argument used in establishing the chronological scheme for the pottery (for Selinus, too, provided crucial evidence in this context):

> *Major Premiss*: We believe that Selinus was founded in 629/8 B.C., which is the date that emerges from Thucydides, our best source;
>
> *Minor Premiss*: The earliest (Corinthian) pottery at Selinus is of the beginning of the Early Ripe Corinthian phase;
>
> *Conclusion*: Ergo, Early Ripe Corinthian must have begun to be produced about 630/625 B.C.

As at Gela, only in a more emphatic way, later evidence was to place this argument under severe strain. A body of material not known to the pioneers who had employed the argument came to light in the storerooms of Palermo Museum twenty-five years after the publication of *Necrocorinthia*. It apparently came from graves at Selinus, and the series began appreciably earlier than the beginning of Early Ripe Corinthian;[18] it suggested, in other words, that the Minor Premiss in the above syllogism was wrong.

What is interesting is the reaction on the part of some archaeologists to this discovery. When a logician discovers that the Minor Premiss in a given syllogism is mistaken, I imagine that he will instantly suspend belief in his conclusion pending reexamination of the argument. This is not what the archaeologists did.[19] They *liked* their conclusion, and they could claim the justification that one or two discoveries from other parts of the Greek world during the intervening twenty-five years had produced results that harmonized with a belief in a date of c. 625 B.C. for the beginning of Early Ripe Corinthian. Rather than give the conclusion up, and assume that the change in style came, after all, a little later (so as to account for the presence of the preceding phase at Selinus), they had recourse to other measures. The case of Selinus differs from those of some other Sicilian colonies in that an alternative date to that of Thucydides, which is arguably as credible, exists in other ancient sources for the foundation of the city: about 650 B.C. Therefore, by jettisoning the Major Premiss (Thucydides' date) as well as the Minor, the conclusion could be kept intact, however precariously. Thucydides could not, after all, be relied on: Selinus was founded around 650 B.C., not in 629/8: and in accordance with the new evidence, Early

18. See G. Vallet and F. Villard, "La Date de fondation de Sélinonte: Les Données Archéologiques," *BCH* 82 (1958): 16–26.

19. An exception is J.-P. Descoeudres, "Die vorklassische Keramik aus dem Gebiet des Westtors," in A. Hurst et al., *Eretria*, vol. 5 (Bern, 1976), 13–58, especially 50–54.

Ripe Corinthian pottery began to be made a generation or so later than the foundation.[20]

The striking thing about this revised version of the argument is not that it is necessarily erroneous, but that it so conspicuously lacks both logical rigor and even the simple instinct for self-preservation. For if we abandon the ship of Thucydides in order to grasp the life belt of Diodorus Siculus, Eusebius, or other later authorities, normally not thought to be of the same reliability in matters of chronology, then we deprive ourselves of the right to use Thucydides' dates in the whole range of western colonial foundations, for some of which we badly need them. In so doing, we inevitably destroy confidence in the chronological structure for Greek pottery, and thus for Greek archaeology as a whole, for the period between about 735 and 580 B.C. These are not perhaps irremediable losses, but it is fair to look around for other possible explanations of the phenomena before we accept them. In fact, to anticipate for a moment, the story turns out to have a conventional happy ending. Further excavations at Selinus have shown that the group of early pots found in the museum at Palermo were an aberrant phenomenon, if indeed their provenience can be relied on at all: the evidence of the settlement and sanctuaries at Selinus, which can be argued to have a more direct bearing on the presence of Greek colonists than that of Greek pottery in the graves, in every ascertainable case begins with the Early Ripe Corinthian phase: thus not only Thucydides' date but also Payne's use of it for chronological purposes seems vindicated.[21]

It is best to let negative criticism rest here, and look instead for such positive lessons as can be learned from the story, bearing in

20. Vallet and Villard (cited above, n. 18). It is significant that they had anticipated the same conclusion, on independent grounds, in their earlier paper, "Les Dates de fondations de Megara Hyblaea et de Syracuse," *BCH* 76 (1952): 318–21.

21. R. Martin, "Histoire de Sélinonte d'après les fouilles récentes," *CRAI* 1977, 46–63, especially 50–51.

mind that the latest episode in it is highly unlikely to be the last. A recurrent message that it conveys to me is the danger of expecting the evidence of excavation to speak to us in the same clear language as that of the historical event. With the case of Selinus, the archaeological evidence has displayed its inherent qualities—particularly incompleteness—in exemplary form, but this has perhaps already been sufficiently illustrated in other instances. More instructive, perhaps, are the examples of ambiguity that have arisen. For, even if we assume that we can satisfy ourselves that a site has yielded some of its very earliest material without having been excavated in its entirety, by what criteria are we going to decide the point at which that site becomes recognizable as a Greek colony? Clearly the occurrence of a single Greek pot in a grave is too little, since that grave may belong to a native non-Greek who acquired the object in the era before colonization; equally clearly, the construction of a monumental Greek temple is too much, in that such an undertaking was only likely once the colony had become firmly established. We may, as we have seen, be led to give differential emphasis to evidence from the settlement and sanctuaries, and evidence from cemeteries. We may let speculation run further, and ask whether we can necessarily assume that the word "colony" (*apoikia*) in our sources has a constant meaning in the material terms with which archaeology must deal. These same questions arise again when we consider other, broader aspects of Greek colonies than their foundation dates.

One such broader question—indeed, perhaps the most fundamental of all—is that of the very existence of a Greek colony. One of the episodes of Greek colonization recorded in our sources (though not this time including Thucydides) is the settlement by the Phokaians of places on the Mediterranean coast of Spain. Two colonies in particular, Mainake and Hemeroskopeion, have proved problematic. If they were really founded from Ionian Phokaia, then general historical considerations make it

very unlikely that they date from after the sixth century B.C; and
in fact the earliest report of their existence, though preserved for
us in a much later work, the *Ora maritima* of Avienus, in most
opinions goes back to a source before 600 B.C. But neither here
nor in later authorities do we find sufficiently precise topographical information to give their exact location: we can hardly go
beyond saying that Mainake lay on the coast east of Malaga,
while Hemeroskopeion lay further round to the northeast, in the
vicinity of Cabo de la Nao, south of Valencia. The trouble is that
extensive exploration of the Spanish coast in both these areas has
failed to reveal any site that looks like an Ionian Greek colony of
Archaic date.

    This is clearly a problem for the archaeologists to solve, and it
is archaeologists who have come forward with proposals, some
of them quite drastic, for a solution. In respect of Mainake, already nearly twenty years ago J.-P. Morel asked whether this had
ever, in reality, been a Phokaian colony;[22] in 1971 M. Tarradell
went further and described both colonies as "phantoms".[23] Now
in a case like this, where the written tradition about the foundations is so much less full and explicit than Thucydides' account
of the Sicilian colonies, we must be careful not to ask too much
of the archaeological evidence: the minimal requirement of a site
with a reasonable quantity of Greek material, going back to the
sixth and preferably to the seventh century B.C., may prove to be
enough. If we adopt such a line of reasoning, then we may look
favorably on the recent proposal of H.-G. Niemeyer, who suggests that Mainake was none other than the *Phoenician* site that
he himself has been excavating for some twenty years past: it was
never, in the strict sense, a Greek colony, but Phokaian settlers
were perhaps tolerated within a much older Phoenician com-

    22. See *PdP* 21 (1966): 391, and, more fully, "L'Expansion phocéenne en
occident," *BCH* 99 (1975): 853–96, especially 886–92.
    23. Cited by J.-P. Morel, "Colonisations d'occident," *MEFR* 84 (1972):
731.

munity, thus giving rise (in Greek eyes) to the notion that this was a Greek city.[24] Niemeyer's view satisfies the minimum requirements stated above, for there is seventh-century Greek pottery on his site. It also underlines one of the points made earlier: the difficulty of distinguishing, in material terms, what exactly was a Greek colony. It is possible, though surely now unlikely, that future exploration will produce an alternative "Mainake" that corresponds more closely to the expectations of the Hellenist; but pending such a find, it seems to me wise to adopt, for the best existing solution of the identification of Mainake and as a principle for approaching the still unsolved problem of Hemeroskopeion, an attitude of liberality towards the archaeological evidence, neither requiring nor expecting too much of it.

Our experience so far may make us hesitant about accepting claims either that the evidence of excavation has substantiated the historical sources or that it has discredited or undermined them. My final example from the field of colonization takes us back to Sicily and to Thucydides, indeed to the passage (6.2.6) that immediately precedes his account of the Greek settlement of the island; but this time it concerns Phoenician, not Greek, colonies.[25] A single sentence conveys the essential information:

> There were Phoenicians living all round Sicily, who had settled on promontories and offshore islands, the better to trade with the Sikels; but when the Greeks arrived in large numbers by sea, they withdrew from most of these places and concentrated in Motya, Solocis, and Panormos, near to the Elymians, both because they trusted in the Elymian alliance, and because from there the sea passage to Carthage is shortest.

It should first be explained that the Sikels and the Elymians

24. H. G. Niemeyer, "Auf der Suche nach Mainake: Der Konflikt zwischen literarischer und archäologischer Überlieferung," *Historia* 29 (1980): 165–89.
25. For a notably balanced discussion of this question, see E. Frézouls, "Une Nouvelle Hypothèse sur la fondation de Carthage," *BCH* 79 (1955): 153–76.

were both peoples already settled in Sicily (according to Thucydides) before the arrival of either Phoenicians or Greeks; and
that the arrival of the first Greeks is specified by him in the ensuing passage as having occurred in 735/4 B.C. Given this information, the sentence can be seen to state or imply four relevant
propositions:

    1. the Phoenicians were settled in Sicily before 735/4 B.C., and
       were to be found especially on promontory and offshore-
       island sites;
    2. they were engaged in trade with the Sikels;
    3. their settlements already included Motya, Soloeis, and Pan-
       ormos (as implied by the word "most," halfway through
       the sentence);
    4. their settlements also included Carthage (implied by the fi-
       nal phrase).

All four propositions have in common the feature that, on the
conventional view at least, they appear eminently testable by archaeology; and all four have indeed been so tested. The results
have been strikingly negative. A number of appropriate sites on
promontories, and on such offshore islands as exist, have been
examined without a single Phoenician object earlier than c. 735
B.C. coming to light. The surprising nature of this result is not, I
think, affected by the intriguing observation that, if applied to
Sardinia instead of Sicily, Thucydides' generalization would fit
the archaeological findings beautifully.[26] Likewise, the location
of the main Sikel settlement areas is well established, and numerous cemeteries of the right period have been excavated, without their producing a single Phoenician artifact such as we
should expect to result from frequent trade exchanges. Again, of
the three specific colonies mentioned by Thucydides, Motya has
been excavated intermittently for more than two generations, yet

26. H. G. Niemeyer, "Die Phönizier und die Mittelmeerwelt im Zeitalter
Homers," *Jahrb. RGZM* 31 (1984): 50.

none of the copious material found can be dated as early as, let alone earlier than, c. 735; and the same is more emphatically true of the less thoroughly explored Soloeis and Panormos. Finally, and in many ways most surprising of all, Carthage has been the scene of excavations by many expeditions of different nationalities, both early and recent, and although one deposit in particular ("Cintas's Chapel") showed every sign of dating from the very earliest days of the settlement, neither here nor elsewhere was there anything that could be shown conclusively to antedate c. 735 B.C.

At first glance (and indeed not only at first glance) it would appear that a positive and circumstantial statement by a major ancient authority has been discredited by the results of excavation. Over the past generation, a variety of expedients have been proposed to accommodate these embarrassing circumstances. But if we recall the lessons of other cases, we shall be inclined to proceed more cautiously, and perhaps even to entertain the notion that the two classes of evidence may, quite simply, not bear closely on each other at all. If, for example, it is difficult for us to identify the material traces of a Greek colony positively, how much more strongly does this apply in the case of a Phoenician trading post? Again, the relative success of archaeology in substantiating the record of Greek colonization in Sicily may actually have obstructed the recovery of the Phoenician record: this would explain the fact, brought out in the article by Niemeyer cited in note 26 above, that in other areas of Phoenician settlement where the Greek material offered no comparable distraction—Sardinia, Malta, Spain, and Morocco, for instance—the archaeological recovery of Phoenician traces has matched or gone beyond the historical tradition, in direct contrast to the Sicilian experience. As for the Phoenician trade with the Sikels, it would not necessarily have been conducted in commodities appropriate for inclusion in Sikel graves; while even Carthage and Motya, of the colonial sites, may have secrets yet undisclosed. In

short, there are explanations that would still allow of a concili-
ation between the historical and archaeological data; and they
may even outnumber those that set up the two classes of evidence
in mutual contradiction.

Insofar as the observations in this chapter have a chronological import, it may be that an opportunity has been missed here:
a concerted attempt could perhaps have been made to advance a
revised chronological scheme for the archaeology of Greece in the
era of colonization. Such an attempt would certainly have been
more positive in effect than much of what I have said. But it could
only be advanced, I think, at the cost of succumbing once again
to the "positivist fallacy": that is, of requiring the evidence of
excavation to express itself in the language of historical narrative. This is the main reason why I have not made common cause
with the two scholars, E. D. Francis and Michael Vickers, who
have recently launched just such a radical project for a new archaeological chronology for Archaic Greece.[27] In their case, the
proposal is to lower, by a margin of anything from one to three
generations, many of the most important dates in Greek archaeology between about 700 and 450 B.C. Much as one may admire
the ingenuity of their arguments (and there are further applica-
tions of them promised for the future), these do seem to me to
rest, as completely as do those of the orthodox view they criti-
cize, on the expectation that major episodes of documented
Greek history are going to be reflected in the material record. It
is this assumption that I have sought to question: in their different ways, the destruction levels at Eretria, the career of the general Leagros, and the reflections in art of the manipulation of the
Theseus legend in Athenian politics—three examples with which

27. The statements of their arguments so far published are "Leagros kalos,"
PCPS 207 (1981): 97–136; "Kaloi, Ostraka and the Wells of Athens," *AJA* 86
(1982): 264; "*Signa priscae artis*: Eretria and Siphnos," *JHS* 103 (1983): 49–
67; and "Greek Geometric Pottery at Hama and Its Implications for Near Eastern Chronology," *Levant* 17 (1985): 131–38.

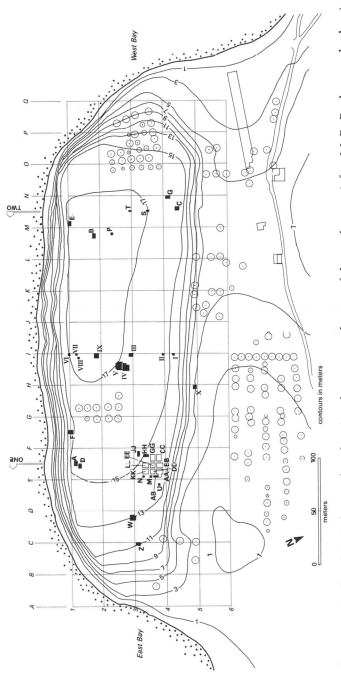

Figure 12. Lefkandi in Euboea: plan showing the excavated areas of the settlement (after M. R. Popham and others).

Xeropolis   Lefkandi   Euboea

Francis and Vickers have dealt in print—are all instances of the kind of episode that, in my view, is unlikely to bridge the gulf between historical and archaeological documentation.

Short of exhaustive discussion, however, this issue remains partly a subjective one. For a final instance from early Greece, therefore, I turn to a case that has some claims to being objectively quantifiable. It concerns the site of Lefkandi in Euboea, which, though not itself a colony, has been repeatedly brought into the discussion of Greek colonization since excavation began there in 1964.[28] The joint Anglo-Greek excavations have not been continuous since that date, however, and circumstances have combined to direct their focus much more on the cemeteries than on the settlement. But the graves found so far have little direct bearing on the colonial period, since they break off well before its beginning, and inferences for eighth-century Lefkandi have to be based on the excavated area of the settlement. The map in Figure 12, published in 1979, shows the extent of the excavated area, which within the main settlement has not since been extended. As will be seen, it is very small in relative terms: on the assumption that the settlement covered the whole of the flat-topped Xeropolis hill, shown by the concentric contours, then something in the region of 2 percent of its extent has been excavated. It is on this basis that all statements of a narrative kind about the involvement of this site in the history (including the colonial history) of eighth-century Greece have been based; and on this basis, too, that the provisional picture of fairly intensive settlement between about 750 and 700 B.C., followed by burning and apparent abandonment, must also rest. It is salutary to remember this map when one reads the often confident statements in the secondary literature (I am not referring to the claims of the excavators themselves, which have been more guarded) about the role of Lefkandi in the events of this critical period, and

28. M. R. Popham, L. H. Sackett, and P. G. Themelis, *Lefkandi*, vol. 1, *The Iron Age* (text: London, 1980; plates: London, 1979), especially pl. 4.

especially about its ultimate fate. In this last connection, it is well to remember also that one or two of the test trenches at Lefkandi did produce a little pottery of much later date, belonging to the sixth century B.C., though its function and context remain unclear.[29] The possibility that further excavation of this site will radically change our interpretation of it is obviously more than a remote speculation. Lefkandi has been perhaps the most important excavation of an Early Iron Age site in Greece since World War II, but this does not yet justify us in referring to it, without qualification, as an excavated site.

If there is any substance in the long series of mostly negative criticisms that I have advanced in this chapter, then it follows that some of the objectives traditionally pursued in classical archaeology, or at least in the archaeology of the early historical era in Greece, have been unattainable ones. I would even be so subversive as to suggest that many excavators, in their heart of hearts, are aware of this: but the external pressures on them, and particularly the pressure to impose the character of definite historical statements on their findings, which "are never comprehensive, never capable of supporting but one interpretation and rest upon complex probabilities,"[30] are too strong to be resisted. After all, even a consideration of the buildings in which we live and work today, and an imagined picture of the archaeological traces that they will leave in a few thousand years' time, can bring home to us how poorly the great historical events of the twentieth century will be reflected in them. Pierre Ducrey of the University of Lausanne has provided an actual example: imagine the reaction of the future excavator of Geneva in, say, 3,000 years' time. He uncovers the ruins of the Grand-Théâtre de Genève, which was in point of fact destroyed by fire on May 1st, 1951. He forms tentative hypotheses, which he tests by excavating some 250 meters away. Here he strikes the ruins of the Bâtiment Electoral,

29. Ibid., 78.
30. Clarke, *Analytical Archaeology* (cited above, n. 3), 12.

burned by another fire on August 4th, 1964. His hypotheses harden; it would be perverse to deny that both destructions were caused by the same historical event; he has the chronological evidence to show that they occurred close together in time; he knows, too, the dates of World War II. We can safely predict the conclusions to which (at least if he follows the practices of twentieth-century classical archaeology) he will come, and it is not without relevance that this will also probably involve him in a clash with the evidence of the contemporary documentary sources.[31] We may laugh at him, but we would do better—at least if we work in classical archaeology—to learn from him. We should remind ourselves that although classical archaeology can excel (as the examples in chapter 1 showed) in revealing man the *maker* with startling clarity, man the *doer* is a different and much more elusive quarry.

31. P. Ducrey, "Menaces sur le passé," *Etudes de Lettres* (1977), pt. 2, 13.

CHAPTER THREE

The Rural Landscape
of Ancient Greece

"The Mediterranean world is a world of town-dwellers"—these were the magisterial opening words of R. G. Collingwood's chapter on towns, in the then standard work on Roman Britain, nearly fifty years ago.[1] It is one of those epigrammatic statements whose truth content is so high that it would be pedantic to quarrel over details. It must also serve as the main justification for a state of affairs long taken for granted: the corresponding urban bias of classical archaeology. The history of excavation in Greece has been a story of the unearthing of cities and towns, of the sanctuaries that in most cases lay within them, and of the graves and cemeteries that belonged to them. This tradition could therefore be justified in terms of historical reality, as well as by pointing to the rewards it has brought. It could also be justified in historiographical terms: to judge from the ancient sources, almost everything worth recording, except for the campaigns and battles, happened in the cities, in their political meeting places, their law courts, their sanctuaries, their markets. To anyone sharing the assumption that what is the business of ancient history is also the business of classical archaeology, it would have followed, until

1. In R. G. Collingwood and J. N. L. Myres, *Roman Britain and the English Settlements* (Oxford, 1936), 186.

recent years, that archaeological fieldwork in Greece must be primarily, if not almost entirely, directed towards urban sites.

That starting assumption has perhaps been called into question in the course of the preceding chapters; but in any case, the study of ancient history in our own generation has concerned itself with a wider range of subjects than those that interested the ancient writers; and some of these wider topics involve the study of rural, at least as much as of urban, life. Agriculture and animal husbandry most obviously exemplify this, and the longer-established study of land ownership has an equally clear application to the rural sector; slavery, technology, and demography also have their rural aspects.

Furthermore, not even the most traditionally minded classical archaeologist will maintain that ancient *historical* texts are the only ones that concern him. There are also the ancient geographers, and beyond them the whole field of literature *sensu stricto*, into which rural life makes persistent, if usually brief, obtrusions. We may take a random example from the opening sentence of a Platonic dialogue: "Have you just come back from the fields, Terpsion, or have you been back a long time?"[2] We note that no third alternative is entertained as a possibility, and we are thus reminded that there is a life going on outside the city walls; only that life has little or no "history" in the conventional sense. Finally, excavation is not the only kind of fieldwork open to the archaeologist in Greece and, even if it were, I could conjure up again the ghost of Wilhelm Dörpfeld tirelessly turning over the soil of the Nidri Plain on Leukas, well away from any documented ancient site (though such laborious methods are neither feasible nor perhaps desirable today).

These are all reasons why the modern archaeologist of Greece, even if he takes a more traditional view than I do of the relationship between archaeology and history, might think of turning his

2. *Theaetetus* 142a.

attention to the rural landscape of Greece in antiquity. But, on the same hypothesis, he may not find so convincing the further argument that will form the main burden of this chapter: namely, that a strong incentive to examining rural ancient Greece is the very fact that our ancient sources do not display much interest in it. Some may question this last claim; others may contest the argument drawn from it; but the claim itself has first to be established.

Let me first make two exclusions so as to be clear as to what this claim does *not* embody. I am not speaking of any lack of response to the beauty of rural scenery: although a case could be maintained at length here, it is not part of my present purpose. Nor am I referring to any dearth of information on the technical practices of agriculture. For the ancient world as a whole, Latin writers more than make amends in both these areas for any earlier deficiencies on the part of Greek authors. I am concerned rather with questions about the *nature* of the ancient rural landscape of Greece: what did it look like, what was its condition in environmental terms, how far was it diversified, how far was it inhabited, and what went on there besides farming? What, in short, can we establish about the economic geography of rural Greece?

There is one empirical argument that can be advanced in support of the view that the ancient writers leave us very much in the dark on such matters. It is to cast our minds back to the days when the ancient writers formed virtually the *only* source of knowledge about rural Greece, ancient or modern. In these days of color photography and relatively easy foreign travel, it may require some effort for us to put ourselves in the position of our predecessors in classical studies, though it should not be too difficult for older readers, particularly those who lacked imaginative or well-traveled teachers, to cast their minds back to their childhoods. Today, most of us can mentally set any reference to the Greek landscape in the context of some sort of picture, at first or second hand, of that landscape as it is today. But of course this was not always so, and if we look back to the age of the Enlightenment, or of the Romantic movement, we can read in the pages of a Keats or a Hölderlin an image in words of the Greek landscape that was derived entirely from readings in ancient authors and contemporary expositions of them. However we allocate the responsibility for it, we must all agree that that image was a profoundly mistaken one.

I am, of course, speaking from the standpoint of a northern European, and, as we shall see, this may be an important consideration. In dealing with the important question of how far the landscape of rural Greece today corresponds with that of antiquity, for example, the botanist Oliver Rackham describes a strand of thought that "arises from Western schoolboys and artists being educated in Classical literature, the setting of which is, unconsciously, transferred to the landscape of their own countries. The French or English visitor . . . expects to see heroes spearing the boar in noble forests and nymphs swimming in crystal fountains; finding instead the tangled prickly-oaks and trickling springs of the real Greece, he infers that the land has gone to the bad since Classical times."[3] The last phrase shows how this delusion has become a serious matter; but first we must acknowledge the truth of Rackham's previous point. That northern Europeans used to envisage the landscape of Greece in terms of that of their own countries can be shown, for example, by the green hills of Calauria and the dripping woods of elm and willow on Tenos traversed by Hölderlin's Hyperion;[4] or by the somewhat absurd environmental settings given by Victorian painters to their classical subjects—as in Waterhouse's *Hylas* (Figure 13), in which every detail would be more appropriate to southern En-

3. O. Rackham, "Observations on the Historical Ecology of Boeotia," *BSA* 78 (1983): 345–46.
4. *Hyperion, oder Der Eremit in Griechenland* (1797–99), ed. J. Schmidt (Frankfurt, 1979), 63 and 16.

Figure 13. *Hylas and the Nymphs* by J. W. Waterhouse.

gland than to Greece.[5] Everyone will agree that such scenes are a travesty of the landscape of Greece *as it is now.* But what of the claim, less easily falsifiable, that it was once, in classical times, much more like this?

This view is a more widespread, respectable, and durable one. Although Rackham advances some substantial arguments for rejecting it, his main conclusion, that the degree of forestation in classical Greece was no greater than today, must rank as unorthodox even in 1983. The traditional view he criticizes derives some of its authority from a famous passage in the *Critias* (111b–c) in which Plato not merely describes the deforestation of Attica in earlier times, but actually spells out some of the accompaniments, such as the loss of rainfall. As Rackham observes, however, the meaning of this passage has been distorted. Plato has

5. On J. W. Waterhouse's *Hylas and the Nymphs*, see Richard Jenkyns, *The Victorians and Ancient Greece* (Oxford, 1980), 190, where he remarks that even the nymphs are "unmistakably English."

been called as a witness for a well-known ecological phenomenon: deforestation leading to erosion on the hill slopes, with all
the ulterior consequences of that. What he *actually* describes is
the reverse sequence, an inexorable and apparently natural denu-
dation or erosion of the mountain soils of Attica, which in turn
caused deforestation by loosening the tree roots. By ignoring a
vital distinction between man-made and natural agencies, scholars have built up a largely theoretical jeremiad of cumulative degradation of the environment. "They have too easily supposed
that a succession of builders of triremes, insouciant shepherds,
marauding armies, Turkish maladministrators, and rapacious
woodcutters—some of whom might otherwise be expected to
undo the damage done by others—have reinforced one another
and each contributed to a progressive decline."[6] This, Rackham
shows, is an improbable reconstruction, presupposing as it does
a single-minded and uninterrupted process of destruction and
making no allowance for the compensating processes of nature.

Plato's words in the *Critias*, on the contrary, show primarily
that, for a thoughtful Athenian of the fourth century B.C. con-
structing a mythical, not literal, account of his country's prehistory, it was *already* reasonable to describe the landscape of Attica
as resembling "the wasted skeleton of a sick man." In other
words, at a point only a quarter of the way through the life of the
historical Greco-Roman culture, Plato's readers could already
recognize the treeless and stony bareness that many modern writers have first deplored and then blamed on the destructive activity of unenlightened (which means primarily post-classical) man-
kind. I find it easier to follow Rackham's view, at least in the
aspect of vegetation cover to which it mainly refers: that we
should assume the rural landscape of ancient Greece to have re-
sembled, in environmental terms, that of Greece today.

The reader who is prepared to share this assumption can then
turn once again to classical literature and, if he looks widely and

6. Rackham, "Observations" (cited in n. 3 above), 346.

closely enough, find many features that will not be unfamiliar. A first point that emerges clearly is that the rural landscape, as today, was differentiated—one might say graded. The commonest distinction in the sources is between the *oikoumenē* and the *eskhata*: between the part of the landscape where people lived, or at least worked, and the other region that existed not only all round the frontiers of Greece itself, but, on a microcosmic scale, round the territory of many individual Greek states—the sector devoted to hunting and pastoralism, warfare, and the training and initiation of the adolescent males. We are also given the impression, though less clearly, that this grading of the landscape was somehow less sharp than what we are used to in the wilder parts of northern Europe and North America. Even the *eskhata* were regularly, if sporadically, used for warfare and other purposes. In ancient as in modern Greece, little if any of the homeland was regarded as a total wilderness. With North America there is, of course, an enormous difference of scale, but this is not true of an area like the Highlands of Scotland. I doubt very much whether there was or is anywhere in Greece where the same thing could happen as occurred forty years ago in Sutherland: during World War II, a military airplane went missing and the searchers, entering the area where it was last reported, found a crashed plane dating from World War I, which had not been seen by anyone in the intervening thirty years. In Greece, one finds the traces of man (including ancient man) almost wherever one goes. For instance, the rocky cliff path that runs round the headland between Aigosthena and Kreusis on the Corinthian gulf, so precipitous that the guerrillas in World War II could, with a modest expenditure of gelignite, close it altogether for long periods, was used by sizeable armies in antiquity, including, on more than one occasion, the marches of King Kleombrotos before he led the last great Spartan army to defeat at Leuktra.

Then there is the question of the pattern of rural landholding. Let us focus for a moment on an image used by Sophokles near the beginning of the *Women of Trachis*. Deianeira, the wife of

Herakles, is complaining that her husband's questing life-style keeps him away from home for long periods. She waits anxiously for his return, and he hardly ever sees his children: "Like a farmer who has taken a distant field into cultivation, and sees it only just when sowing and harvesting" (32–33).

This image must have been at least as vivid for Sophokles' audience as it is for us—more so, if we live in more northerly climes, since it describes a kind of farming not normally possible there. Sophokles was himself a landowner and (even if the play was actually produced after the Archidamian War had broken out, as is possible) probably three-quarters of the audience had firsthand experience of agriculture themselves. To this day, one can see pieces of marginal land in Greece that *look* as if they have been treated in the way this image describes, and some kind of crop still comes up; whereas away from the Mediterranean, there are always activities (winter plowing, fertilizing, weeding) that need to take place at periods other than seedtime and harvest. Thus even a dramatic poet can conjure up a glimpse of rural life.

But there is one further piece of information that may be squeezed out of this Sophokles passage, brief though it is. It seems to me to give the clear impression that the outlying field is at some distance from the farmer's other land. Now, one of the constants all modern anthropological, economic, and juristic studies of Greece take almost for granted is the system of land-ownership. A given farmer's landholdings are likely to be a number of small plots widely scattered over the landscape (Figure 14). Inasmuch as this is the direct result of the modern Greek system of partible inheritance, and inasmuch as there is clear evidence of the existence of a similar system in large areas of ancient Greece, it would seem to follow that an ancient Greek farmer, too, had to cope with this extraordinarily inconvenient circumstance. Most ancient written sources, assuming their readers' familiarity with such matters, tell us relatively little about this in direct words, though there are inferences to be drawn from the Attic orators, for example. It is therefore valuable to find Soph-

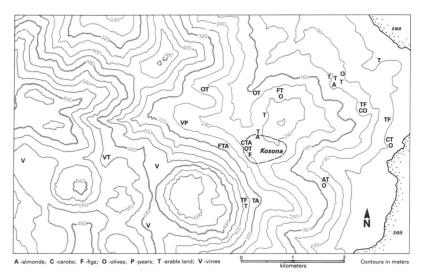

A -almonds; C -carobs; F -figs; O -olives; P -pears; T -arable land; V -vines   Contours in meters

Figure 14. Map showing the landholdings of a single family in the Methana peninsula (Argolid) in 1976 (after H. A. Forbes).

okles implying the existence of such a system in fifth-century Athens.

But this interpretation of a poetic metaphor may already seem too literal-minded to some readers, so I shall turn instead to the place where we might naturally look first for full descriptions of the rural landscape: that is, to what might loosely be termed the geographers. I do so with hesitation, because there are many who know more than I about such writers, and I am also conscious of following, in fairly close succession, the learned Sather Lectures of Christian Habicht on Pausanias.[7] But, as will become clearer in the next chapter, I have in the past six years had intensive experience of at least one region of rural Greece, Boeotia, in the course of carrying out an archaeological survey there, and this

7. See, now, Christian Habicht, *Pausanias' Guide to Ancient Greece*, Sather Classical Lectures, vol. 50 (Berkeley and Los Angeles, 1985). I thank Professor Habicht very warmly for his generous loan, during my stay in Berkeley, of the then unpublished typescript of his lectures.

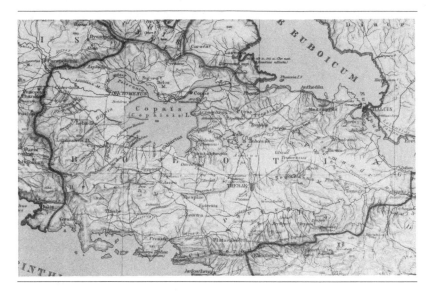

Figure 15. Map of ancient Boeotia (after W. Kiepert).

has involved the study of the ancient geographical texts. It is in fact on the ancient landscape of Boeotia (Figure 15) that I shall concentrate, beginning with the fullest surviving ancient treatment of it, the ninth book of Pausanias's *Description of Greece*, written in the third quarter of the second century of the Christian era.

Let me try to anticipate one criticism by saying that, whatever the exact purpose for which Pausanias wrote his book was (and that is not quite so simple a question as it might seem), I fully appreciate that he was *not* setting out to throw light on the kinds of question that concern us here, so that it is unfair to tax him with omissions in this area. He evidently set out to describe the things most worth seeing in the mainland of Greece for the benefit of the reasonably well informed and intelligent traveler of the Roman imperial period. Most of his readers would doubtless have shared his own presupposition that this meant, almost exclusively, the monuments of Greece's noble past, rather than of its subdued present; and they would quite certainly have shared his further assumption that the most interesting sights were, by and large, to be found in and around the cities. Pausanias does not, in any case, ignore the landscape outside the cities: on the contrary, he has a definite eye for certain kinds of natural feature. But I shall still argue that, for him, the rural landscape is largely a kind of void that intervenes between each city or sanctuary and its nearest neighbor; a void crossed by the lifeline of the road system (doubtless much improved under Roman rule), which enabled the traveler to pursue a linear course from starting point to destination, with little regard for the lateral and vertical dimensions. But, as often, it is better to exemplify than to generalize.

Let us then turn to the opening chapters of book 9, and see how Pausanias conducts his reader through Boeotia. He has already explained in his account of Attica (1.38.8) that Mount Kithaeron was "the border of Boeotia," and he takes this up at 9.2.1, where he speaks of part of Kithaeron (the northern slopes, we are left to infer) being "Plataean ground." He gives, in passing, an interesting glimpse of the agricultural practices of the Plataeans, though in the context of the years round 373 B.C. (9.1.3): in their justified suspicion of the Thebans, the Plataeans at this period did not venture out into their more outlying fields unless they had reason to think that a political assembly was being held in Thebes, which would occupy the attention of the Theban citizen army. This same historical narrative gives him occasion to mention that there were two alternative roads, one more direct than the other, from Plataea to Thebes, and presently he will himself introduce us to both of them (9.2.1, 3). Before even entering Plataea, he makes a first detour to Hysiai and Erythrai, and then characteristically retraces his steps. Each feature that he mentions is related to the road he is following ("on your right as you turn off"; "on your right on the way back"). There follows his description of Plataea, and then, at 9.4.4, we are on our way again. Our destination is Thebes, but it is not made clear (and the omission has cost gallons of modern ink) whether Pausanias's mention of the spring Gargaphia, in the immediately preceding sentence, implies that it lay on or near this road (the spring had been one of the main landmarks in the famous battle of 479 B.C.).

As we follow Pausanias to Thebes, it is helpful to know that, in Boeotia as elsewhere in ancient Greece, many place-names were held to derive from the names of mythical personalities: thus, Plataea from the nymph Plataia, a daughter of the king Asopos who gave his name to a river, and who was supposed to have been a successor of a king Kithaeron who gave his name to the mountain, and so on. All this Pausanias faithfully reports (9.1.2). But consider his description of the next stage of the road:

> On the way from Plataea to Thebes is the river Oeroë; they say Oeroë was a daughter of Asopos. Before you cross the Asopos, if you turn downstream for forty stades [i.e., about eight kilometers], you come to the ruins of Skolos. . . . To this day, the river Asopos divides the territory of Plataea from that of Thebes.

Note that we are not given an overall distance (though we are told the length of the detour to Skolos). Pausanias makes it clear enough that you come to the river Oeroë before the river Asopos, but the careless reader might well take his story of the relationship between their two eponyms to imply that the former river is a tributary of the latter. This is not so: one flows westwards and the other eastwards. As for the Skolos detour, it has generated a long debate as to whether this sentence allows, or excludes, the possibility of Skolos itself, though reached by turning down the near bank of the river, lying on the far (i.e, northern) bank. In some opinions the likeliest site for Skolos, at the right distance from the main road, lies on the north bank.[8] This is one of the many topographical disputes arising from the fact that one can-

8. See W. K. Pritchett, *Studies in Ancient Greek Topography*, vol. 1 (Berkeley and Los Angeles, 1965), 107–9; vol. 2 (1969), 178–80.

not be *sure* that Pausanias has mentioned every significant detail; though as a matter of fact, any sort of firsthand familiarity with the Greek landscape, such as would give one a true picture of the small size and volume of such rivers as the Asopos, might lead one to doubt whether the crossing of such a stream would constitute a "significant" step.

It may seem less than just to contrast Pausanias with a man who has been called "the prince of travelers," but a comparison of his account with that of William Martin Leake, who traversed the same road rather more than sixteen centuries later, will bring out some of what I miss in the former. Leake leaves Plataea with an initial detour in the opposite (i.e., southern) direction:

> *Dec. 29, 1805.* From the upper angle of the ruins [i.e., of Plataea] I ride in twenty-three minutes, preceded by a man on foot, over the rocky slope of Cithaeron to the fountain Vergutiani, and thence ascend in five minutes to a projecting rock now serving as a shelter for cattle, in the middle of a natural theatre of rocks at the head of the verdant slope above the fountain. . . . Having descended from the fountain into the road which leads from Kokkla eastwards to the villages along the mountain side, I cross the branch of the Oeroë which, coming from Thebes, I called the first, and eight minutes further a hollow, the waters of which form a branch of the Asopus; its upper extremity is very near the sources of the easternmost branch of the Oeroë. Here, therefore, is exactly the partition of the waters flowing on the one side to the sea of Euboea, on the other to the Corinthiac Gulf.[9]

Notice how Leake first of all sets the season for his journey, an important detail for all questions of the level of lakes, the flow rate of rivers, the snow line, and so forth. Notice his use of orientation. Notice how phrases like "the verdant slope" or "a shelter for cattle" evoke both the landscape and its uses, besides mak-

9. W. M. Leake, *Travels in Northern Greece*, vol. 2 (1835), 326.

ing it easy for us to follow in his tracks. Notice his unwavering precision over journey times, making it possible to calculate distances. Notice finally how clearly he settles the matter of the direction of flow of the two rivers that arose in connection with Pausanias.

Despite obvious differences of purpose and background, there are many similarities between Pausanias and Leake. Both describe Greece primarily in terms of the traces of earlier periods; both do so with learning and honesty, and in a way that often makes us want to follow in their footsteps. Above all, both are supremely self-effacing: Pausanias would no more think of inserting into his account of the battle of Plataea the fact that he himself bore the same name as the victorious commander than Leake would of mentioning the day—presumably some time during the month of November 1805—when he received news of the battle of Trafalgar (although it had a certain relevance to his mission, which was to carry out a confidential survey of the geography of Greece, partly with a view to defending it against the French if the clash between the two powers spread there). The little that we know of Pausanias himself emerges entirely from a few casual hints dropped in the text of his book, and it is not much exceeded by what Leake reveals of his own views in his work. Finally, both men timed their journeys outstandingly well, Pausanias for the description of standing buildings that were soon to collapse, Leake for the detection of their remains before many of these were to vanish too.

But, from the excerpts that we have seen, it is the differences of approach that emerge more conspicuously. Leake, partly because of his mission, is more interested than Pausanias in the Greece of his own day; and he is perhaps typically British in relishing, or at least taking an interest in, the rural scene. But my motive for setting up the comparison between Pausanias and Leake is really to show that there is a possible alternative to the former's approach; and that the outlook and interests of a Pausanias need not be regarded as permanently binding upon the archaeologist of Greece.

We do not need to follow Pausanias's description of Boeotia sentence by sentence: much of the essential information can be conveyed by means of a map (Figure 16) containing *only* such information as he gives in his account, though incorporating one or two necessary principles, such as that of including the approximate compass directions, which are absent from his pages. In chapter 8 he at last enters Thebes, which he will use as the center for his three subsequent excursions into the Boeotian territory. Ten chapters are occupied with the description of the city itself. Then he embarks on the first excursion, which turns out to take us roughly northeastwards to the shore of the Euripos opposite Euboea, and occupies chapters 18 to 22 inclusive. The black circular symbols mark the towns (or more often the ruins of towns)

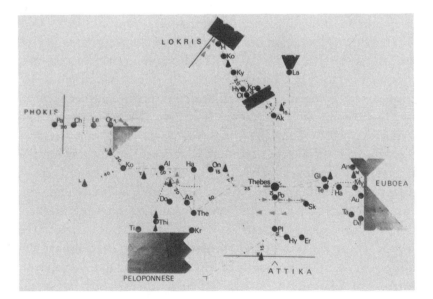

Figure 16. Map of ancient Boeotia, containing only information taken from book 9 of Pausanias's *Description of Greece.*

that he passes through; black conical symbols are mountains, gray conical symbols rivers, with their direction of flow (also usually omitted by him); the sea, where he touches it, and the portions of lakes that he mentions, are shown by the gray areas, while dotted lines mark the few cases where he mentions territorial boundaries. Distance figures are intermittent, and the fragmentary appearance of the map as a whole reflects the virtual absence of *lateral* cross-references: for instance, in saying whether the coast reached on one journey is the same one as that reached at a different point on an earlier or later journey. On the first, eastward excursion, the omission of a distance figure has again led to difficulty in locating a site, Teumessos (TE). A little further on, at Mykalessos (MY), there is a curious crux raised by Pausanias's reference to a sanctuary of Demeter "by the sea of [or at] Mykalessos," when other evidence makes it impossible to believe that Mykalessos was on the coast.[10] The fault here (if such it can be called) lies in a failure to distinguish between a town itself and an outlying part of its former territory.

The second excursion occupies but two chapters (23 and 24), and starts from the same gate of Thebes, on its eastern side. Yet, though Thebes was fabled for its possession of seven gates, we prove to be going in a quite different direction, rather west of north, to reach the Euripos again at two places, Larymna and Halai. As before, Pausanias makes detours but always retraces his steps to the main route of the excursion. The journey has the interest of including a boat crossing of an arm of Lake Kopais, between Akraiphnion and Kopai: here above all we would welcome an indication of the season of the journey, since it is unlikely that this area was more than seasonally covered by the lake in the second century A.D. One may remark on (some indeed have deplored) Pausanias's omission of any mention of the Mycenaean fortress of Gla, and a further difficulty arises when Pausanias

10. J. G. Frazer, *Pausanias' Description of Greece*, vol. 5 (London, 1898), 66–70, gives what is still the fullest account of this matter.

gives distance figures between two pairs of towns—eleven stades from Kopai to Olmones, seven from Olmones to Hyettos— which are improbably small, the second being well under a mile. Since the first and third of these places are definitely located, we can in fact state that either a textual corruption or a thoughtless error has occurred.[11]

The third and last excursion, which takes Pausanias out of Boeotia and into Phokis, starts from a different gate of Thebes and runs approximately westwards. It is much the longest, covering chapters 25 to 41 inclusive. It differs from its predecessors in its disjointedness: we start in the usual way by going as far as Onchestos, then retracing our steps for part of the way and turning off to Thespiai, the second main tourist attraction in ancient Boeotia. But then there are two abrupt leaps in space: first we jump to Kreusis, "the harbor of the Thespians," which we learn can be reached from the Peloponnese by an unpleasant zigzag voyage round headlands. We are therefore on the Corinthian Gulf, and no doubt Pausanias visited this part of Boeotia on a separate journey by ship. From Kreusis, we sail westwards to the harbor of Thisbe, visit Thisbe itself, and then proceed to Tipha. This poses the most substantial topographic puzzle in the book: both the harbor of Thisbe and Tipha have been located, and there is no question but that, if sailing westwards, you would come to Tipha before and not after Thisbe.[12] The best explanation lies in the realization that a linear progression like Pausanias's does not have to be in a *straight* line: both Tipha and Thisbe lie within a deep bay, and Pausanias's course must have curved round and

11. See R. Etienne and D. Knoepfler, *Hyettos de Béotie et la chronologie des archontes fédéraux entre 250 et 171 avant J.-C.* (*BCH* suppl. 3, 1976), 3–4, 19–29.

12. See R. A. Tomlinson and J. M. Fossey, "Ancient Remains on Mt. Mavrovouni, South Boeotia," *BSA* 65 (1970): 243–63, with a different explanation for Pausanias's sequence, 243 n. 2; and on the place in general, E.-L. Schwandner, "Die boötische Hafenstadt Siphai," *AA* (1977), 513–51.

doubled back on itself after he entered the bay, although he does not tell us so.

There follows the second leap in space, the most abrupt of all. At 9.32.5 we are suddenly told: "Inland from Thespiai lies Haliartos." It is more than four chapters since we left Thespiai, but what is more trying is that this move brings us within a bare two miles of a point that we reached even before that (9.26.4)—the sanctuary of Onchestos, which some travelers must have been surprised to find themselves in full view of without having been told of its proximity. From Haliartos, we go westwards to Koroneia and Orchomenos, again passing Lake Kopais, which however is only mentioned because in winter the south wind carries its waters over the territory of Orchomenos. We leave Boeotia by way of the towns of Aspledon, Lebadeia, and Chaeroneia, although in order to visit these places in this order from Orchomenos, one has to pursue a tortuous itinerary that would involve some retracing of steps.

What I hope mainly to have conveyed by this extensive summary of Pausanias's route through Boeotia is its relentless *linearity* (the interruptions notwithstanding). His treatment of the landscape is for much of the time in one dimension: each place is further or nearer along the line of the road that he is following; when he makes a detour, he retraces his steps; different roads are not related to each other laterally, and not even three-term relations along a single road ("*B* is between *A* and *C*") are used. Few if any orientations are given, and changes or reversals of direction are sometimes left for the reader to infer. The image that springs to mind is that of a man crossing a morass on lines of duckboards who does not venture on short cuts. It is interesting to find that Christian Jacob has suggested[13] that Pausanias may have habitually used, not a proper two-dimensional map, but an

13. C. Jacob, "Paysages hantés et jardins merveilleux," *L'Ethnographie* 76 (1981–82): 41.

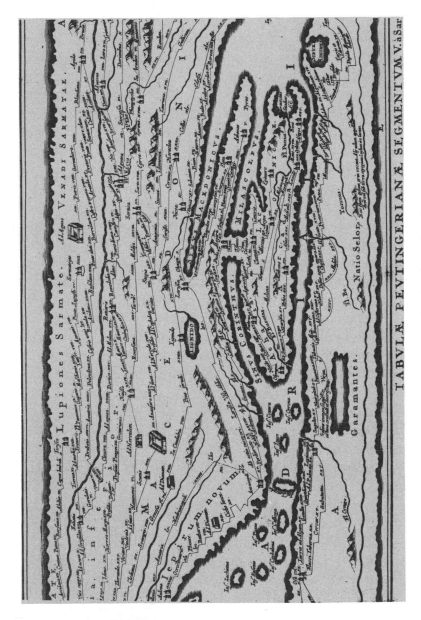

Figure 17. Detail from the *Tabula Peutingeriana*: the Greek peninsula.

itinerary of the kind of which one precious example is preserved for us in the Peutinger Table (Figure 17), a thirteenth-century copy of a "world map" of about A.D. 300 that displays almost exactly the same kind of linearity, concentrating on progress forwards to the point where lateral relations become not only neglected but distorted (in Figure 17, for example, the position of Boeotia is at two quite different points along the two separate itineraries that lead to Athens).

I do not dissent from Jacob's view that Pausanias's topographical indications are nevertheless, in the main, effective for the traveler who shares his interests, though instances like the silence over the proximity of Onchestos and Haliartos are perhaps exceptions. But in a treatment such as Pausanias's, the rural landscape cannot really emerge as a two-dimensional space. There are a few signs of interest in the rural scene, mostly directed at natural phenomena (as in the description of Mount Helikon), and on one occasion actually referring to landscape use (in the short but fascinating passage on the flood-control measures taken in the landlocked basin that lies between Thisbe and its harbor). But rural settlement, population, and agriculture are passed over in silence, requiring as they do an awareness of rural *space*.

To the obvious objection that I have unfairly imposed modern concerns on an ancient writer, and then compounded the offense by comparing him with a modern one, I reply by introducing a quite different comparison, with two earlier writers, Strabo and the author who for long went under the misleading appellation of pseudo-Dikaiarchos. Strabo, like Pausanias a Greek-speaking subject of the Roman Empire from Asia Minor, compiled his *Geography* over a longish period, beginning nearly two centuries before Pausanias. By comparison with the latter, he starts with one signal disadvantage: whereas no one can dispute the immediacy of some of Pausanias's firsthand descriptions, "it is not possible to say with certainty whether Strabo ever saw any part of

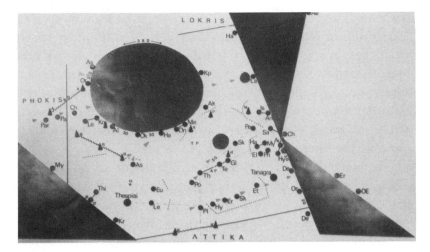

Figure 18. Map of ancient Boeotia, containing only information taken from book 9.2 of Strabo's *Geography*.

Boeotia";[14] and similar doubts hang over other sections of his account of the Mediterranean world.

Once we look at Strabo's Boeotia, however, through the medium of a map (Figure 18) corresponding to the earlier one for Pausanias, we find certain qualities that were missing in the other's case. Strabo uses orientations; his Boeotia has two continuous coasts, and includes more features and places than are mentioned by Pausanias. The measurements that Strabo gives are not only linear ones along roads, but also cover distances across the sea (as between Boeotia and Euboea), and include a figure for the periphery of Lake Kopais. This last is always the hardest kind of measurement to calculate, and Strabo's surprisingly high figure may be based on a painstaking coverage of every promontory and inlet: if so, it is the more impressive to find topographical work of this level being undertaken. Towns are given a rough grading according to size and prosperity.

Strabo does not, like Pausanias, undertake his journeys radi-

14. P. Wallace, *Strabo's Description of Boeotia* (Heidelberg, 1979), 1; cf. 168–72.

ally from Thebes; his purpose is different, even though his own
description of what he is doing, *periēgēsis tēs chōras*, precisely
recalls Pausanias's title for *his* work. Strabo's original plan is to
cover the landscape by treating it as a series of regional groupings
of towns and villages; the trouble is that he does not stick to this
plan. After an exemplary account of the northeastern seaboard
(9.2.6 onwards), he reasonably turns to the inland plains (9.2.15)
and describes them. But then (9.2.21) he abruptly switches to using the long entry in the Homeric Catalogue of Ships (*Iliad*
2.494–516) as the basis of his account. The result is, as Paul Wallace observes, most unfortunate: the sequence of places in Homer is governed more by considerations of meter than by those
of topography, and Strabo's hitherto coherent sequence falls
apart.[15] Even so, his account is more continuous than that of Pausanias, and his interest in natural features is deeper and more systematic. What he offers us is, in short, a true *physical* geography;
in this respect, the rural landscape is covered in a degree of detail
that roughly corresponds to Pausanias's much fuller description
of the urban scene. In cases where actual autopsy is important to
the issue—as with the discrepancy over the disappearance
(Strabo 9.2.33) or the survival (Pausanias 9.26.5, at a later
date)—of the grove of Poseidon mentioned by Homer at Onchestos, we have good reason to trust Pausanias more. But there
is a common negative feature of both accounts: Strabo, even in
the first and more systematic part of his description, exhibits no
more interest than Pausanias in the landscape as a field for, and
in part the product of, human activity. On the *economic* geography of the countryside, both authors are essentially silent.

   But is the whole search for information of this kind miscon-
ceived? Is it simply a product of anachronistic modern precon-
ceptions? Surprisingly, perhaps, we are able to give a firm negative answer: there exists a little evidence to show that there *were*
authors and readers in ancient Greece who shared, to some de-

   15. Ibid., 3.

gree, the concerns that have dominated this chapter. It is refreshing to turn to a third account of Boeotia that, although hasty and, in both senses of the word, partial, displays just such interests, and thus fills some of the gaps in Strabo's and Pausanias's descriptions. It is hard to believe that a writer whose work was once described by Wilamowitz as being almost without rival in the extant body of Greek literature for its richness of life, should have met with the relative neglect that has been the fate of Herakleides *ho kritikos* (or possibly *ho Krētikos*, the Cretan). His three surviving fragments were much discussed in the years between their detailed examination by Müller in *Fragmenta Historicorum Graecorum* in 1848 and the end of the nineteenth century; but since then there has been little, apart from the monograph Friedrich Pfister devoted to them in 1951.[16] In brief, because the fragments appeared in two manuscripts set among works ascribed to the philosopher Dikaiarchos, their author for years passed under the guise of "pseudo-Dikaiarchos." It seems to have been F. Osann, in 1831, who first noticed that Apollonius, a Hellenistic writer on marvels, gave an almost verbatim quotation from one of these fragments, and ascribed it to an otherwise quite unknown Herakleides Kritikos. Much study was devoted to the dating of the fragments on their internal evidence: the upshot is that we can place them firmly within the time-span of 275–200 B.C., and more tentatively between c. 260 and 229 (perhaps even between 260 and 251 B.C.). Their author thus antedates Strabo by about the same margin as Strabo does Pausanias. We are concerned here only with fragment 1, an itinerary that proceeds from Athens to Chalkis by way of eastern and central Boeotia.

It is instantly clear that we are in the presence of an individualist and a humorist: quotations, off-the-cuff evaluative judg-

16. F. Pfister, *Die Reisebilder des Herakleides*, Sitzungsberichte, Österreichische Akademie der Wissenschaften, Philosophisch-Historische Klasse, no. 227, vol. 2 (Vienna, 1951), especially 17 (Osann's identification of the author), 44–48 (his date), and 45 (citation of Wilamowitz).

ments (often derogatory), and downright gibes alternate with extremely observant description. Thus, as we set out on the road into Boeotia from Oropos:

> From here to Tanagra it is 130 stades. The road runs through a landscape of olive groves and forest, entirely free of any fear of robbers. The town lies on a rocky eminence, with a white, clayey appearance, much beautified by the house porches with their votive pictures in encaustic technique. It is not particularly rich in locally grown produce, but its wine is the best in Boeotia.

This passage is quite typical. When Herakleides arrives at a town, he is mostly interested in describing the character and behavior of the people (particularly the women), often entertainingly. But it is his passages between the towns that are the revelation. Thus, from Tanagra to Plataea, "the road is lonely and stony, stretching out along Kithaeron"; from Plataea to Thebes, it is "smooth and level." Thebes is placed in its environment: the city is built "on black earth"; "well-watered, green, with deep soil, it has the most gardens of any city in Greece." These features, he goes on, and the abundance of local produce on sale, make it a pleasant summer resort; but in winter it is windy, snowy, and muddy. From Thebes to Anthedon, the road is "oblique but driveable, running through fields." Anthedon has trees planted in its marketplace; rich in wine and seafood, it lacks corn because of the poverty of its soil; nearly everyone there is a fisherman, and many build their own boats. As for the land, it is not that the Anthedonians neglect it, but that they simply do not have it.

We could do with a lot more information of this kind. But at this point, to our dismay, our author pronounces: "That is what Boeotia is like. For Thespiai has ambitious menfolk, fine statues, and nothing else" (this last being apparently his apology for omitting to visit a major point of interest in Boeotia). There follows a barrage of devastating anti-Boeotian apophthegms, ending with Pherekrates' "Keep away from Boeotia if you are wise." We realize that, besides Thespiai, Herakleides is not going to take us to Koroneia, Orchomenos, or anywhere west of Thebes, and our only consolation is his parting description of the road along the shore from Anthedon to Chalkis, between the wooded, well-watered hills and the sea. The rarity of such description among Greek writers merely sharpens our sense of deprivation.

Such, at least, is my reaction. The existence of this fragmentary work proves that such an approach to the study of rural Greece could exist in antiquity; for even if Herakleides is dismissed as not being a "serious" author, his writings must have interested a certain readership. But more important is the fact that the virtual isolation of the work, in respect of its subject matter, among the surviving ancient sources means that, in pursuing the same approach today, we cannot use these sources as a framework. We shall, to be sure, be able to glean both information and insights from the literature—sometimes, as we have seen already, in rather unexpected places—but these will mostly come in fragmented form; we can, in a somewhat different way, use "universalizing" texts (for Bocotia, Hesiod's *Works and Days* is the obvious example) to extract and apply more specific conclusions; but for much of the time, we shall inevitably be on our own.

Today, however, that will hardly constitute an argument against pursuing a line of archaeological enquiry—nor, for that matter, of historical enquiry. The true justification for studying rural ancient Greece is indeed, in a broad sense, historical. Once again, I cite the verdict of an earlier Sather lecturer, Moses Finley, in one of the central conclusions of his *The Ancient Economy*. Finley found that the view of the ancient city as primarily a center of consumption, founded on the work of Max Weber, was justified. He concluded that the survival of the city accordingly depended on four main variables; first among these was "the

amount of local agricultural production, that is, of the produce
of the city's own rural area."[17] This, to me, is justification
enough. The archaeologist who pursues the study of rural
Greece, rather than accepting the urban focus of interest of the
ancient sources as a kind of datum, will in fact be probing beneath the surface of this "world of town-dwellers," and examining its economic underpinning. To establish a means of imple-
menting this aim will be the task of the next chapter.

17. *The Ancient Economy* (Berkeley and Los Angeles, 1973), 139.

CHAPTER FOUR

The Rural Landscape of Greece Today

TO RESCUE FOR HUMAN SOCIETY
THE NATIVE VALUES OF RURAL LIFE

Inscription on Hilgard Hall,
University of California, Berkeley.

These words, carved perhaps seventy years ago, are apt to sound either sentimental or affected in the 1980s. Yet, passing under the inscription nearly every day for more than three months, I developed a growing sympathy with the aspiration that it expresses. Field archaeologists working in Greece are indeed inclined to wax sentimental over the rural environments in which they often find themselves, but this does, I think, reflect a genuine attachment. It is certainly true that a number of archaeologists today are engaged, if not in rescuing, at any rate in studying the contemporary rural values of Greece, with a view to using them in their reconstructions of the ancient counterparts.

In modern times, the Greek countryside has successively been the victim of a series of processes, each destructive in its different way. Many Western visitors seem to see it and its inhabitants as a kind of living museum, and find it difficult to treat the modern Greek villager as a contemporary, let alone an equal. For the small subgroup of the Western visitors who are professionally interested in its past, the landscape itself is often seen as a sad and mistreated relic of a different and superior past. I considered this view in the previous chapter and found certain grounds for thinking it a misrepresentation. The history of the view, if correctly

93

reconstructed, certainly supports that conclusion: it grew up with the flowering of classical studies in northern Europe, and it embodied not only a conjectural picture of the past landscape, but also a definitely mistaken impression of the contemporary one. When experience proved the falsity of the latter element, a way presented itself of salvaging what remained: the "true" landscape of Greece could still exist, provided that it did so only in the past.

I can write of this view, not as a disdainful onlooker, but as a former adherent, at least in part. An education that combines relative familiarity with the ancient texts and total ignorance of the physical realities is no longer a common experience for young people today, at least in the Western world; but I can recall my own feelings of shock more than thirty years ago on first encountering the real Mediterranean landscape, first of Italy and then of Greece. The standard translations into English of the Greek vocabulary for nature—terms like *hulē* (wood), *bēssa* (wooded glen), *potamos* (river), *krēnē* (fountain), and *poa* (grass), and their Latin counterparts—had been downright misleading as a preparation for confronting the actual features denoted by this vocabulary. Was it *possible* that this muddy trickle corresponded to that historic river-name? Where had the green glades with their nightingales gone? As we saw in chapter 3, an explanation lay to hand, simple, apparently credible, and attractive above all to the classicist: the landscape described by the classical poets and historians had vanished with them, the victim of environmental degradation, and consequent climatic deterioration, in the post-classical era. This is in many ways a comforting view, and may not be mistaken in its entirety: to prove it so would require much more extensive research than has yet been undertaken. All that I argued in chapter 3 was that it has no great basis or justification in the ancient authors; that the findings of modern research into the question are inconclusive; and that, as a more economical working hypothesis, we should instead adopt the opposite assumption, that the ancient rural landscape of Greece was, in many important aspects, much like that of Greece today.

Or at least, of Greece yesterday: for we come now to the latest of the processes of destruction—this time in a literal, not symbolic, sense—that the Greek countryside has suffered. The physical degradation of the rural environment, which is now a subject of worldwide concern, has not spared Greece. On the contrary, although tact and a consciousness of sentimental nostalgia urge reticence upon me, I do not recall seeing a more intense and apparently unchecked manifestation of this disease of our times anywhere else in the world. The spread of surburban building and second homes, the ubiquitous replacement of stone and brick by concrete, the paths of destruction left by the tractor and the bulldozer, the neglect or demolition of terracing, the idiosyncrasies of Greek planning and taxation legislation, and, above all, the universal dumping of refuse in an age of plastics, have all contributed to a degradation that is more than merely visual. This catalogue must not be allowed to degenerate into a tirade: it should be remembered that not all these processes are in themselves undesirable, and admitted that many of them are, in practical terms, irreversible.

Yet there is one minor side effect of this process that is acutely relevant to our present topic: the increasing pace of destruction of antiquities in rural sites. Here, curiously, the action of the law, which in other respects is recognized by everyone (including successive Greek governments) as being too permissive, even supportive of environmental damage, has the opposite effect. Because Greek antiquity law imposes a blanket prohibition on the destruction of ancient remains until they have been professionally investigated, a direct clash of interests has been set up between government agency and majority public opinion. This in turn has brought a trail of unhappy consequences: a spate of clandestine building, a detectable change in the popular attitude to Greece's archaeological heritage, and a massive addition to the burdens laid on the Archaeological Service. It is neither my business nor my aim to argue contemporary political questions; but it is open to anyone to wonder how long the present balance of forces can remain unchanged, and it is not difficult to diagnose the underlying cause of the trouble in theoretical terms. If there is one glaring ideological contrast between ancient and modern Greece, it is the change in, indeed the inversion of, the relative evaluation of public and private interests. The language that gave us the word *idiot* and its derivatives to describe the man who stood aside from public life now employs these terms freely in a neutral or occasionally commendatory sense, most often to warn trespassers off private property. The rural landscape is a mute witness to the fact that this change of values is no mere philosophical abstraction.

All of this lends a certain urgency to the questions that I shall raise about the form of future archaeological work in Greece; but it is not the only practical consideration operating to that effect. I have referred in passing to the difficulties under which the Greek Archaeological Service labors, and I hope that it will not seem too presumptuous to enlarge on them a little. The unselective preservation of Greece's material heritage, which is a cause so estimable in principle that almost nobody would speak in public against it, has brought about another, less obvious crisis. The historically conscious visitor to Greece today is rightly impressed by the steady increase in the number of local museums and in the quality of exhibition. What he or she may not appreciate—and I think that this is true even of classicists and other "professionals" who are not archaeologists—is that what is actually displayed is merely the beautiful tip of an unsightly iceberg. Almost every museum in Greece is compelled to conceal in its storerooms a mass, growing year by year at an alarming pace, of material unsuited to exhibition, which is often unpublished and sometimes destined to remain so. If the Archaeological Service were rewarded, either in salaries or in manpower, on a scale that bore some faint relation to the colossal indirect contribution that its activities make to the nation's tourist industry, then one could look ahead to a possible reduction of the pressure. As things are, the only prospect is that it will rapidly increase: even to keep pace with the rate of growth in the "submerged nine-tenths" of its holdings, the service would need an appreciable increase in manpower. Much of the material has to be stored in improvised accommodation, difficult of access for study; meanwhile, its keepers are distracted by the ever more persistent demands of emergency excavation, generated by the factors already mentioned.

The activities of the foreign missions in Greece make a contribution towards shouldering one of the burdens, through their undertaking rescue excavations when asked. But, since they must necessarily share the same museum facilities, they inevitably aggravate the other main burden, by adding to the growth of the unseen *"apothēkē* [storeroom] mountain." The problem is not peculiar to Greece but, because of the exceptional richness of Greece's archaeological heritage, it appears there in its acutest form. Any excavation, even that of a ten-meter square undertaken to prepare the way for the building of a modest office block in a provincial town, is likely to produce a significant crop of material from a variety of periods, spanning millennia rather than centuries. Some answer to the problem has to be found in the near future: the option of a total moratorium on all but emergency excavations, which used to exist only in the context of examination papers for classical students, begins to move in the direction of serious possibility. It is time to ask ourselves whether our appetite for new objects, connoted by the invocation "*Kala vrēmata!*" ("Good finds!"), which is still regularly heard at international gatherings of archaeologists, is something that can be allowed to be satisfied indefinitely. Can it not, perhaps, be separated from the appetite, entirely justifiable and indeed desirable, for new *knowledge*?

If accepted, several of the arguments used in earlier chapters would tend to limit the value of the traditional aims of excavation in Greece. These, like earlier comments published by me in this vein, are bound to arouse resentment in some circles. It is clear, for one thing, that a general adoption of the *ethos* of the new archaeology in Greece would result in an alteration of the balance between the two entities just mentioned: new objects and new knowledge. A concrete instance is available from the past twenty years of fieldwork in Greece, from the publication of the results of survey and excavation by the University of Minnesota Expedition in Messenia (and, one might add, from the reception of that publication). This work has undoubtedly generated new knowledge in a very much higher ratio to preserved finds than has elsewhere been the rule. For an appraisal of the verdicts on this project, I turn to the first place where anyone would look for a really candid assessment of anything new in the archaeology of the eastern Mediterranean: that is, to a review by James D. Muhly. "Nichoria," he writes of the site chosen for test excavation after the expedition's survey work had been completed, "is perhaps the most eroded site ever to be excavated in Greece. . . . If Nichoria had been excavated in the traditional manner, by archaeologists interested in monumental architecture and museum-quality artifacts, the result would have been an utter disaster." In the event, what we have is an extremely informative excavation report to add to the earlier publication of the results of the survey. Muhly warns that: "There is one very unfortunate consequence of this. Nichoria will, in the minds of many scholars, confirm a deeply held belief that the 'New Archaeology' . . . is an archaeology of last resort, something undertaken when all else fails. In the words of one of its critics, it is the archaeology you do when you do not find anything." He goes on to exemplify such a reaction: "When one has the frescoes of Akrotiri who is going to bother collecting soil samples?" But the sting is in the tail: "It is precisely the lack of proper scientific excavation at Akrotiri that is responsible for most of the nonsense published about Thera during the past ten years."[1] I should like to associate myself with every word of these opinions: it is pleasant to feel that one has at least one ally and sharer in the retribution that awaits those who express views of this kind.

There is one branch of archaeological work—in some senses, it is an application of the new archaeology—that has the effect of bringing together almost all the strands of argument that I have deployed in this chapter and its three predecessors. It offers classical archaeologists a chance to make use of the distinctive strengths of their own discipline, but in a way that will only be fruitful if they work in collaboration with the practitioners of other disciplines. It enables them to contribute substantially to a different branch of historical study from the traditional, event-oriented political one, and to do this on the scale, not of a single, restricted locality, the site, but of a *region*. It explores the rural sector of ancient Greek life on which our ancient sources are most defective, and corrects the urban bias of the past century and more of excavation in Greece. It generates relatively little in the way of preserved finds, but an almost endlessly exploitable store of new knowledge. It is (as many readers will long since have guessed) intensive archaeological field survey. The excavation of Nichoria, which we considered just now, was primarily the by-product of the first great pioneering survey venture in Greece, the Minnesota Expedition of the 1960s. A series of further projects, mostly on a more modest geographical scale, has followed the lead of the Minnesota team, but the application of

1. J. D. Muhly, review of *Excavations at Nichoria in Southwest Greece*, vol. 1, *AJA* 84 (1980): 101–2.

this technique to the exceptional circumstances of Greek archaeology must still be reckoned to be in the experimental stage. Shortcomings and downright errors are still likely to occur. But one further advantage of survey as a method is that such shortcomings and errors can be made good later, in a way impossible with the essentially destructive technique of excavation. A stretch of terrain can be surveyed again and again at suitable intervals, whether by the original team or by others, to check on the original results. The processes of nature and the agricultural activities of man, which are responsible in the first place for bringing to the surface the archaeological material from which field surveys obtain their information, will continue to operate everywhere except where external destructive forces have prevented them from doing so.

But I have preferred to exemplify rather than generalize, and in line with this I now propose to offer a small selection of the findings of the Cambridge/Bradford Boeotian Expedition, which since 1979 has been jointly directed by John Bintliff of the University of Bradford and myself, with the help of colleagues and students of several disciplines from both these universities, and from others as well.[2] I have tried to prepare the ground somewhat in the previous chapter by setting out the picture of the rural landscape of Boeotia obtained from those ancient sources that give the fullest account of that region; this formed the background against which we began our work. As we saw, the picture is a meager one, even though Boeotia fares as well as most regions of Greece in this respect. The example of the fragment of Herakleides Kritikos showed us that the approach of the writers of antiquity did not, in principle, preclude them from giving us valuable information in this quarter; rather, it is the vagaries of survival

2. The reader is referred to an extensive preliminary report entitled "The Cambridge/Bradford Boeotian Expedition: The First Four Years," *Journal of Field Archaeology* 12 (1985): 123–62, for a more detailed account of the questions raised in this chapter.

Figures 19, 20. Two views of field teams carrying out intensive survey in Boeotia, 1981.

of texts that has left us with so bare a picture of the rural economic geography of ancient Greece. But, as it happened, the part of Boeotia where we elected to work was not one that Herakleides described: it embraces parts of the ancient territories of the cities of Thespiai and Haliartos, where the two abutted. Herakleides found a contemptuous pretext for not troubling to visit the former place, and mentioned the latter only as a byword for the stupidity of its inhabitants.

Our coverage of the terrain has been as intensive as that attempted in any part of the Mediterranean world, or so we believe; for this reason, our progress has been relatively slow, and the area surveyed in the five seasons to date amounts to less than thirty-five square kilometers. Figures 19 and 20 exemplify some of the conditions with which field survey in Greece must reckon. A harvested cornfield, where a team of five or six people can move in a straight line and in clear view of one another, may invite smooth and rapid progress; yet the conditions under foot, with a stubble and straw cover, will demand extremely careful examination of the surface if anything is to be seen. Conversely, a well-kept vineyard or freshly ploughed ground under olive trees will make it very difficult for the team to preserve its alignment and orientation, yet the walkers' view of the ground surface immediately in front of them may be almost complete, and show up each artifact perfectly. Allowance must be made for these and other factors when estimating the significance of the visible scatter of material on the surface, and before venturing to infer its relationship with what lies under the ground.

These problematic aspects of surface survey have led some archaeologists to take a very skeptical view of the potential contribution of the technique as a whole. Others have doubted the specific value of the *intensive* variety of survey I am describing. More productive, in their view, is the selective coverage of a much larger tract of land, in which the likely locations for sites are identified in advance, and then examined at close quarters for surface traces. Each side in this latter debate can advance persuasive arguments of an a priori kind, with considerations of thoroughness and objectivity on the one side being weighed against those of productivity and historical significance on the other. It will be obvious that intensive survey is very much more laborious and expensive in proportion to the size of the area examined than is survey of the second, "extensive" kind. For us, the decisive factor in making the choice is an empirical finding of the simplest kind: in every case where intensive survey has been attempted in Greece, it has revealed a density of sites on the landscape that is very much higher—at times, by a factor of fifty or more—than that revealed by surveys of the extensive kind. (In Greece, the extensive survey projects were mostly a feature of the pioneer years in the 1960s and early 1970s, while most of the more recent projects have been intensive; Figure 21 shows, on a logarithmic scale, the magnitude of the change in site recovery that has come about with this adoption of new tactics.)

Now this result may appear predictable, to the point of leaden-footed banality. But it poses a searching question to the expo-

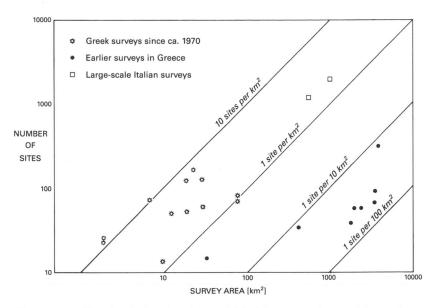

Figure 21. Graph of site densities yielded by extensive and intensive surveys in Greece (after J. F. Cherry).

nents of the extensive approach. It means that there is *something* there on the ground, capable of being revealed if the terrain is searched in its entirety, but unlikely to be discovered by the extensive method, or any other selective mode of investigation. We shall presently be going into the question of the significance, indeed the reality, of the pattern of "sites" that the intensive surveys claim to have unveiled, but whatever the outcome of that examination, it seems to me that to exclude the recovery of such patterns from the outset can only be justified if their historical significance is negligible or nonexistent. It will, I think, prove difficult to maintain such a point of view for very long.

At this point, it will be useful to consult again Figure 15, a map taken from an authoritative classical atlas, showing the picture of the relevant part of ancient Greece that can be gleaned from other sources. As is apparent, the density of place-names is low and the detail (apart from timeless natural features) minimal. If it be objected that this map dates from 1906, one may reply that an up-to-date version would, for the classical period the map purports to illustrate, have very little indeed to add. A similar rejoinder could be given to a plea for a larger-scale map: there would be no further details to be inserted. The only substantial class of further information one could include would be that yielded by modern archaeological work, and this would have to be expressed mainly by symbols, since many of the locations have no known ancient name attached to them. We have seen in the previous chapter the explanation for this state of affairs: the knowledge and interests of the ancient writers, on whom the compilation of such maps depends, do not extend to giving a detailed picture of any part of the rural landscape of Greece, unless it chances to have been the setting of a major battle or campaign.

When we compare this with Figure 22, a modern map of the same region, a difference emerges. The modern map is of course greatly simplified, and includes only a small proportion of the toponyms in current use and the features that could be included if the scale were larger. Nevertheless, it incorporates a distinctly higher number of settlements, more closely spaced, than the ancient map. This difference would be easily explained if the population in antiquity had been much lower, or concentrated into fewer and larger settlements (or both) than is the case today. Yet there are strong grounds for thinking that, at least for this part of ancient Greece, neither of these explanations is valid; and our own work has only served to add to these grounds. As a consequence, one might predict that the ancient landscape held a number of as yet undiscovered settlements, perhaps of the same general order as the modern villages with their populations of between one and three thousand, perhaps smaller and more scattered; some might be places as substantial as certain of those whose names and locations we happen to know, and that consequently appear on the map. One part of our purpose was to search for such settlements.

As things stood early in 1984, when the series of maps that follows was drawn, the area covered by our survey took the shape

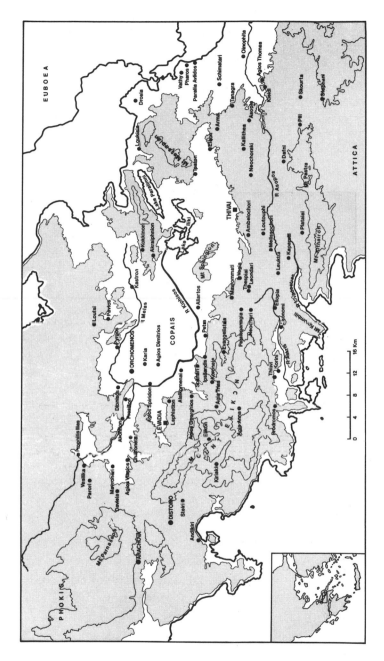

Figure 22. Map of modern Boeotia.

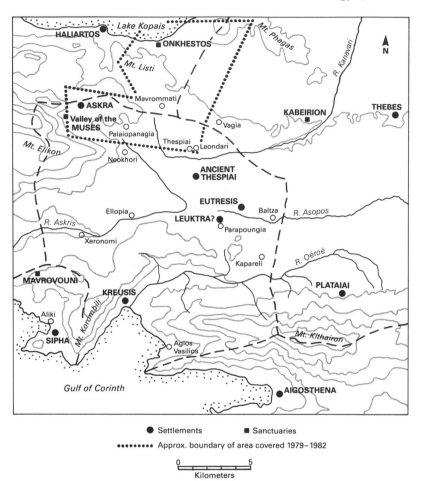

Figure 23. Boeotia survey: location map of area under study.

of a large reversed L in west-central Boeotia, with the vertical
arm running from the edge of the Kopais basin near Onchestos
in the north, almost to the site of ancient Thespiai in the south;
from the latter, a horizontal arm ran westwards up the Valley of
the Muses almost to its head. This block of land (Figure 23) extended into the ancient territories of two, or possibly three, of the
cities that belonged to the Boeotian League: the northern part of

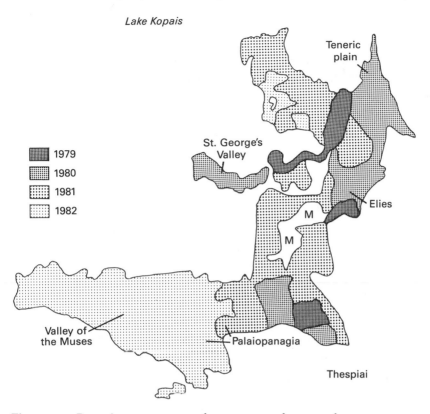

Figure 24. Boeotia survey: annual coverage and nomenclature, 1979–82.

the vertical arm lies at least in part on ground that belonged to Haliartos; the southern section of this arm, and the whole of the horizontal arm, is in the territory of Thespiai; and a small sector towards the northeast may at times have been in the western extremity of the land of Thebes. The last-named was easily the largest and most powerful city of ancient Boeotia, but Thespiai too was a major power, and its urban center lies much closer at hand. Figure 24 shows the annual progression of our survey across this tract, always extending outwards in a contiguous block of land,

centered on the modern village of Mavrommati, which has
served as our base.

Figure 25 shows the distribution of prehistoric sites found,
ranging over the period of more than 3,000 years from the Late
Neolithic to the dawn of the historical period in Greece. The distribution is both thin and patchy, perhaps suspiciously so. There
appears to have been a long, if intermittent, tradition of settlement in the low-lying area at our northern extremity, close to the
edge of the Kopais basin. A second, somewhat denser, nucleus of
settlement lies to the southwest, on the land over 1,000 feet
above sea level in the Valley of the Muses; but the intervening
space seems empty. Thus far—that is, in relation to its uneven-
ness—there is a case for thinking that this distribution may reflect the realities of the prehistoric settlement pattern; but the arguments involved are of some complexity, centered round the
questions of climate and of preferred agricultural land in prehistoric times, and perhaps relating also to the partial draining of
the Kopais basin in the later part of the Bronze Age, and they are
not directly relevant to our purpose here. But the overall thinness
of the distribution is another matter, and here we suspect that the
realities may not be fully reflected in our results. The probable
reasons have to do with the whole nature of surface survey. Most
laymen are surprised to hear that visible traces of ancient settlements, recoverable without excavation, are to be found on the
modern land surface of Greece. That this should be so of even
earlier periods is yet more surprising, considering the many centuries of more intense activity that have elapsed in the interval.
It is the activities of the plow, with other agricultural operations,
that are responsible for these visible traces, and these will not
normally penetrate more than a short distance beneath the present surface. For the prehistoric land surfaces to have been pene-
trated, lying as they often do several feet below the modern level,
we may be in part dependent on classical cultivators who min-
gled prehistoric material with their own debris; some small remnant of that prehistoric material may survive, along with the later

Figures 25, 26, 27, 28. Boeotia survey: four maps showing site distribution of Prehistoric, Archaic to Early Hellenistic, Late Hellenistic to Early Roman, and Late Roman periods.

evidence, to be visible today. But this is likely to yield only an incomplete picture of the prehistoric settlement pattern, and we suspect that some prehistoric sites lie entirely hidden under the soil, at least in cases where their location did not happen to coincide with settlements, or intensive farming activity, of the historical period.

The relative scarcity of our prehistoric sites becomes apparent once one makes the comparison with Figure 26, a map of the settlements covering the period between approximately 600 and

200 B.C., that is the Archaic, Classical, and early Hellenistic eras. Here is a period when, on any account, population was at a higher level than at any stage of prehistory, but on the other hand it covers a vastly shorter span of time. What is immediately striking is the high, though not absolutely even, density of sites across the landscape. In the area of only twenty-one square kilometers covered by these maps, there are some sixty-six definable sites of this epoch alone; and in a further season of work in 1984, both the density of sites in general and the overwhelming preponderance of this period were maintained, with the total rising to over a hundred. The great majority of these sites can definitely be stated to have been occupied over a narrower time-span, the fifth and fourth centuries B.C., whether or not their life extended earlier and later too.

The next significant feature is one that is not apparent from the map: the very small average size of these "sites." About two-thirds of them are represented by a scatter of material that is half a hectare (5,000 square meters) or less in area: that is, equivalent to a square of about 70 meters by 70, or a circle with a radius of just under 40 meters. When the debris of a settlement, even after some natural dispersal, covers so small an area, this imposes strict limitations on the interpretation of the nature of such a "site." To this, one of the most interesting of the questions raised by archaeological survey, we shall return presently. Meanwhile, it would be reasonable to ask how we establish the existence and nature of what we call our sites.

Intensive survey means the coverage of a landscape, or of a carefully chosen sample of a landscape, in its totality, as far as that can be achieved. Inevitably, there are some insurmountable barriers created by nature, or by the conditions of the present day: cliffs, impenetrable vegetation, and the presence of modern housing or of enclosed land. These apart, our aim has been to cover every piece of ground, at a level of intensity fixed by spacing the field walkers at the maximum interval that will still allow nothing of significance to slip through the mesh (Figures 19, 20).

After a period of experimentation, we found that in normal conditions this interval was fifteen meters. The team counts every pre-modern artifact that is noted, over the entire landscape. For much of the time, the counts are low, though seldom nonexistent; a sudden increase in density indicates the potential proximity of a site, and at this point we halve the interval between walkers, so as to conduct a total count of everything visible on the surface, rather than merely what is within each walker's view. If the density level is judged to confirm the presence of a site, then the team advances in very small rectangles, ten meters by thirty, until the whole area of high density has been covered and its boundaries defined on all sides (Figure 29). The most scientific procedure might seem to be to fix an absolute density level as constituting a "site"; but one thing that survey has taught us is that there are great variations in the "background" density of finds away from the sites, according to the type of landscape over which we are walking. This fact suggested to us that the "site" level should instead be defined *relatively* to this "background" level. This might appear to be a worryingly subjective method, but the plain fact is that in an area of rich "background," whole stretches of terrain attain a density of finds that would be taken to constitute a site in a "poor" area; yet within them lie nuclei of much higher density still. It is reassuring that in all areas we find *relative* concentrations of finds of the same order of magnitude in extent and with the same classes of material represented. Clearly, different levels of intensity in occupation and in agricultural operations, whether in antiquity or more recently, are producing differential traces on the landscape. We are content to interpret the concentrations of finds that we thus encounter as sites.

Two commodities are invariably found in profusion at such locations: potsherds and fragments of roof tile. Occasionally the outlines of buried structures are visible, but more often there are only isolated stones, which may be recognizable as detached building blocks. Even without excavation, the presence of under-

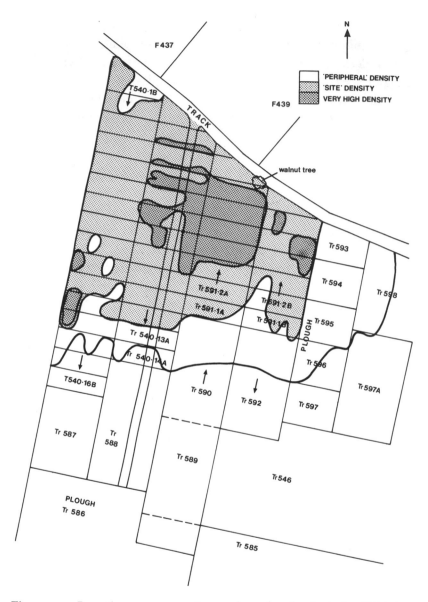

Figure 29. Boeotia survey: specimen plan of a classical site ("Palaio-panagia 7," 1981).

lying structures can be confirmed by the use of geophysical survey, with the aid of an instrument measuring the resistivity of the earth that has been successfully employed on a number of our sites. It will give an indication of the visual impression conveyed by a site if I record the fact that a major settlement, in an area of intense occupation, can produce from twenty to fifty pieces of sherd or tile *per square meter*. Clearly, when this happens there is no difficulty in confirming that a location of past settlement, or at least concentrated activity, has been found. In other cases, the decision may prove more difficult. But there is one other factor that has been of the greatest utility in establishing the reality of our sites: it is the fact, already mentioned by implication, that the great majority of the sites give advance warning of their proximity to the field teams through the existence of a "halo" of finds surrounding the actual nucleus, with a density lower than that of the site itself, but markedly higher than most of the "background." It is seldom that we find such a halo without a site at the center of it, and, conversely, the small class of sites that lack such a halo calls for a special explanation. When a density map of the whole area is prepared (as in Figure 30), the nature of the "halos" becomes apparent: they form an added argument for believing in the reality of the sites. Opinions differ as to the historical causes that have generated these halos (for they have often been encountered in survey work elsewhere). Are they no more than the result of the dispersing action of modern plowing, spreading a nucleus of ancient material across a somewhat wider area? Careful experiment has shown that this is unlikely to be the main explanation, let alone the whole truth: more probably, they are mainly the consequence of the *ancient* agricultural process of manuring the infield area round the site, with fragments of tile and sherd being carried along with the manure. Thus, for example, sherd scatters of much more recent historical periods in Britain have been found to correlate with the areas known to have been under cultivation at the period in question, and to be

Figure 30. Boeotia survey: total density map of artifacts in the Valley of the Muses, Palaiopanagia, and Thespiai areas, 1979–82.

absent from known areas of woodland or heath.[3] We thus learn one further fact about our sites: that they usually formed the foci of intensive ancient cultivation.

One advantage of surveying in Greece, as against other regions of prehistoric and ancient settlement, is that there is a relatively accurate chronology of pottery styles that enables one to confirm not only the existence of a site but the main period or periods of its occupation. Thus one can trace the changes in the settlement of a given area through time, comparing for example the high density of sites in the period from the Archaic to the early Hellenistic with the lower density of the period of approximately equal duration that immediately followed: between roughly 200 B.C. and A.D. 200 (Figure 27). Many complications still arise when one seeks to combine the temporal and the spatial dimensions in this way. One must allow for the possibility that the sites of one period, though more numerous, may be smaller in average size than those of another. Our method of subdividing each site into a multiplicity of small components enables us to cope with this factor, at least to some extent. More problematic is the possibility that a scattered rural population may later have been concentrated in an urban center without any fall in total numbers; here the next logical step is to extend one's survey to cover known ancient city sites, as we propose to do. But in the particular case of the two periods under consideration, when all possible allowance has been made for such factors, the conclusion still emerges that the whole level of human activity in our part of rural Boeotia fell markedly.

Here once again the archaeologist working in Greece can draw on the peculiar advantages of his position and appeal to a series of literary authorities whose statements, sometimes applied to Greece as a whole, sometimes to Boeotia specifically, reinforce the impression that the findings of the survey correspond to eco-

3. See T. M. Williamson, "The Roman Countryside: Settlement and Agriculture in North West Essex," *Britannia* 15 (1984): 228.

nomic reality. One of the earliest indications comes with the warnings of Isokrates in the fourth century B.C. about the impoverishment of Greece as a whole and the growth of a class of wandering, landless people. More specific reports appear in later authors: Polybius, in the second century, writes of the depopulation and the fall of agricultural production in Greece (36.17.5), and in another passage describes the especially acute symptoms of economic breakdown in Boeotia (20. 4–6). As for Strabo and Pausanias, whose accounts we considered in chapter 3, the striking feature of both their descriptions of Boeotia is that they present town after town as being deserted altogether under Roman rule, or at least drastically reduced from its former size and status. These authorities of course span a long period of time, and are not all equally reliable; it is satisfying, therefore, that independent glimpses can be obtained from more specific documents, such as the second-century B.C. Boeotian inscriptions prescribing measures to combat grain shortages. There seems little to contradict the picture that is emerging, in which the changing face of the landscape revealed by our survey is matched by accounts of shrinking or deserted country towns, with all that that implies about the decline in cultivation.

The picture would be incomplete, however, if no reference were made to its quite unexpected sequel: unexpected because, this time, there is little documentary evidence to prepare us for it, and what there is maintains a generally pessimistic tone. For the fact that emerges from our survey—and it is now confirmed by the findings of certain other fieldwork in quite different parts of Greece—is that, some time around A.D. 300, a great revival in rural settlement took place, one sustained until at least the sixth century of the Christian era (Figure 28). The number of rural sites returns to something approaching the level of the Classical and early Hellenistic periods and, even more interestingly, the individual locations chosen for this revival were in most cases the very same ones that had been occupied in the earlier epoch, and then abandoned for some centuries. This probably means that the old buildings, however ruinous, were still partially preserved, and that it was easier to rehabilitate them than to build afresh. In many ways, the fourth to sixth centuries of the Christian era form the second most intensive period of exploitation of the landscape in the whole five-thousand-year history of this part of Greece.

We come now to the most central and important question of all, at least for the period of classical antiquity: how are we to interpret the nature and function of the sites that we have located? Let us recapitulate their main characteristics: they are mostly very small, and often spaced at an interval of only a few hundred meters from one another. They produce quantities of pottery, which in nearly all cases includes household pottery in coarser fabrics as well as painted ware. They also virtually always produce roof tiles, showing that they incorporated permanent structures. Finally, the existence of a "halo" surrounding nearly all of them suggests that intensive cultivation, especially in the immediate vicinity of the site, was a concomitant feature of their occupation.

This combination of features has suggested to us the provisional conclusion that most of our sites were independent farmsteads. It remains provisional because of a number of difficulties that stand in the way of this hypothesis. We may begin with the most general ground for objection: this picture of a populated landscape is not what one might expect to find in the "world of town-dwellers" that belongs to the Mediterranean area. It is not, for example, characteristic of certain post-classical periods (leaving the question of prehistoric times on one side), and it is emphatically not the picture of the landscape of Boeotia today, when virtually the entire population is concentrated into villages and towns and, except at peak harvest periods, the countryside becomes totally deserted at dusk. Then there are more specific problems, of which I shall enumerate three. First, there is the fact that the sites still appear in the immediate approaches of the city: it may be recalled that the site of ancient Thespiai lies only just off the southern edge of the maps shown in Figures 25–28 above. What advantage would a landowner derive from living on his property if it lay within such easy commuting distance of the city? Secondly, there is the question raised near the beginning of chapter 3 about the system of land inheritance: if it is really true that in ancient Greece, as today, an individual's landed property was likely to be divided into a number of small, widely separated parcels, then permanent residence on any one of these might, logistically speaking, be even more disadvantageous than living in the city. Thirdly, we should recognize that not even the possession of a tiled roof would necessarily designate an ancient (or modern) building as being for *human* occupation; nor, even if it were, would the occupants need to be the owner and his family, rather than tenants, slaves, or a bailiff. These "compromise" solutions should all be borne in mind as possibilities, together with the suggestion of second residences for people who also had a house in the city: let us recall, in this last connection, Plato's prescription in the *Laws* (746e) of two houses for each of the 5,040 citizens of his ideal state, with the second one being located towards the outer extremities of the city's territory.

As far as the nonarchaeological evidence on this matter is concerned, we can cite epigraphic evidence for the existence, especially in Hellenistic Boeotia, of permanent and even fairly valuable structures on plots of land outside the city.[4] But the words used to denote these buildings—*aulē* is one of the commonest— are neither very specific nor (as is the way with ancient Greek

---

4. For examples in the territory of Thespiai, see M. Feyel, "Etudes d'épigraphie béotienne," *BCH* 60 (1936): 175–83, 389–415, especially 179, lines 29, 34, and 38; 182, lines 24–26; 394 n. 1; and 397–400, 403, and 413. Particularly helpful is E. Cavaignac's discussion of an inscription earlier published by M. Holleaux, "Prix de terres dans la Grèce et l'Asie Mineure," *REG* 66 (1953): 95–99. The text from Hyettos (see above, Feyel, 394 n. 1) is further discussed by R. Etienne and D. Knoepfler, *Hyettos de Béotie et la chronologie des archontes fédéraux entre 250 et 171 avant J.-C.* (*BCH* suppl. 3, 1976), 244 n. 911. For an example from Thisbe, see *IG* 7.2225, line 25.

terminology) invariable in their meaning.[5] They could perfectly
well, for example, describe animal shelters temporarily shared by
human occupants at times of peak agricultural activity (thus explaining the household pottery), round which would be concentrated vegetable plots or other intensive cultivation (thus explaining the "halo" of dense sherd cover generated by manuring).
The question is unlikely to be settled without fresh kinds of evidence. Even so, the mere existence of these structures, in the periods where they occur, is enough to show that the countryside
of this part of Boeotia must have worn a very different look from
its appearance today, when one may walk for several kilometers
across the landscape without coming across a single permanent
building outside the villages.

By way of contrast, it is worth saying a word about the very
small group of sites that possess quite different features, and to
which probably none of the explanations considered above can
apply. They are smaller even than our average "farmstead" sites;
they do not normally have a conspicuous "halo" around them;
and the pottery that they produce is well above the average, both
in respect of its original quality and in that of its present preservation, seldom including any coarse ware at all. As professionals
may already have guessed, we interpret these as small rural grave
plots or cemeteries, some of whose burials have been disturbed
by relatively recent cultivation. But their location, sometimes in
decidedly out-of-the-way spots, may one day be brought to bear
on the broader questions of landholding and residence that we
have been discussing.

In terms of Greek history, and indeed of Greek literature, it is
however a handful of our larger sites that is likely to arouse wider
interest. We have in fact found half a dozen classical sites of well
above the standard size, ranging for the most part between two

5. As shown by R. G. Osborne, "Buildings and Residence on the Land in
Classical and Hellenistic Greece: The Epigraphic Evidence," *BSA* 80 (1985):
119–28.

and five hectares in area, and three of these merit special reference. First, there is the site we call "Plains B2." Over two hectares in size, it contains a number of dressed building stones, and it has produced three examples of something infrequently found in surface surveys, namely inscribed potsherds. All are too fragmentary to produce informative readings, but by their mere existence they suggest the interpretation of the site as a sanctuary, where dedications of any kind might be inscribed. The site lies at the northern edge of the Teneric Plain, and is just under a kilometer to the east of the known site of the sanctuary of Poseidon at Onchestos (of which, indeed, it may be no more than an outlying and subsidiary element); a short distance northeastwards again lies the Mountain of the Sphinx, whose location can be fixed from literary sources. In this general area, Pausanias (9.26.5) mentions a sanctuary of Herakles the Horse-Binder (*Hippodetēs*), which has never been definitely located. Albert Schachter, the foremost expert on Boeotian cults, has suggested to us the possibility that this sanctuary could be our site.[6] There is the difficulty that Pausanias, coming from the east, mentions it as coming *before* the Mountain of the Sphinx, which is "further on," but we have perhaps considered Pausanias's methods sufficiently in the previous chapter to show that this is not an absolutely conclusive objection, although it is still awkward.

At a similar distance on the far, western side of Poseidon's sanctuary at Onchestos lies another, even bigger classical site, which we have called "Plains A5." Here we have found no inscriptions, but there is the biggest concentration of building stones that has occurred anywhere in our area, including a piece of a Doric cornice; furthermore, within the area of the site a small Greek excavation in 1973 had brought to light what appeared to be an *agora*, or civic center, of the Hellenistic period. This site,

6. But W. Judeich, in "Das Kabirenheiligtum bei Theben, i," *AM* 13 (1888): 85–86, suggested a different site, somewhat further east and on the opposite (southern) side of the Teneric Plain.

whose surface area was about five hectares, was surely a small urban center. Here we are able to suggest something that runs counter to orthodox interpretation: when Pausanias visits Onchestos, he finds what he describes as *poleōs ereipia Onchēstou*, the ruins of the *city* of Onchestos, adding that in his day the temple and statue of Poseidon, together with (as we saw in chapter 3) the sacred grove of trees, still survived. Now his use of the word *polis* has been taken, since the days of J. G. Frazer, to have been loose: he is simply referring to the conglomeration of buildings that would arise around any major sanctuary. We now propose that he meant the word in a stricter sense: there *was* after all a town of Onchestos, otherwise hardly recorded in history and certainly not an independent city (it lay within the territory of Haliartos), but still an urban center. This would also explain why Herakleides Kritikos, in the catalogue of the localized vices of Boeotia that forms the parting salvo of his description, includes Onchestos in what is otherwise a list of nine major Boeotian cities.[7]

For our third site, we move southwards and uphill to the Valley of the Muses (Figure 31). For us this has always been, in more than one sense of the word, sacred ground. It is, first of all, by far the densest area of rural settlement that we have encountered. Not only are the sites relatively large and numerous, but the "background" level of finds between the sites remains at an almost continuously high level along the valley floor. Partly because it lies well over 1,000 feet above sea level, it is also the pleasantest area for summer walking, as well as the most scenic, that we have seen in Boeotia. It is, too, the prime wine-growing locality of the region round Thespiai; fine trees, perennial streams and springs, and high-quality land help to make up a delightful landscape (Figures 32–33). The overall density plot of finds in this part of our survey, included in Figure 30, throws some kind

7. F. Pfister, *Die Reisebilder des Herakleides*, Sitzungsberichte, Österreichische Akademie der Wissenschaften, Philosophisch-Historische Klasse, no. 227, vol. 2 (Vienna, 1951), 180, 183.

Figure 31. Panoramic view of the Valley of the Muses, Boeotia, from the south side.

Figure 32. Valley of the Muses: view eastwards down the valley from the Pyrgaki Tower.

Figure 33. Valley of the Muses: view southwestwards into the upper valley, from the Pyrgaki Tower.

Figure 34. View of the tower and the outer fortification, on the summit of the Pyrgaki Hill.

of objective light on this quality. Three or four distinct sites were already known in the valley when we came to it: the Sanctuary of the Muses itself, at the head of the more or less level part of the valley shown in Figure 33; the late classical or early Hellenistic watchtower that crowns the hill called Pyrgaki on the north side (shown at the far left of Figure 31, and forming the vantage point from which the photographs in Figures 32 and 33 were taken), and which has usually been taken to be the one mentioned by Pausanias as being the only surviving trace, in his day, of Askra, the home village of the poet Hesiod (Figure 34 shows a closer view of the tower itself); another tower, this time of the Frankish period—probably the thirteenth century of our era— crowning the lower hill called Palaiovoro (Figure 31, center; Figure 32, left); and the church of Agios Nikolaos, high up on the southern side of the valley, where in 1806 Leake found and copied an important inscription about the athletic festival associated with the Sanctuary of the Muses (*IG* 7. 1776), which led him, uncharacteristically, into the error of thinking that the sanctuary itself was there.[8]

One question that we had especially hoped to settle was that of the exact site of Hesiod's village of Askra. It was always hard to believe that the tower on top of the bleak Pyrgaki hill, some 2,150 feet up (Figure 34), marked the site of the actual settlement. It was therefore interesting to find that at the eastern foot of this hill there lay easily the biggest and densest site of our region so far discovered: some twenty hectares in extent, it was far too big to be covered in its entirety by our most intensive procedures and had to be handled by means of a sampling process. Particularly interesting was its chronology: the prehistoric era apart, the earliest sherds from here date to around 900 B.C.; occupation then seems to have been fairly continuous until the earlier Roman imperial age; then there is a gap, corresponding neatly to the time of Pausanias when, in his words, "one tower and nothing more was left of Askra to remember it by." There follows the seemingly inevitable resettlement in the fourth century A.D., continuing into the Byzantine and Turkish periods, before the locality reverted to the cultivation of grain and vines. Nor was this site unusual only in its size: at two periods, the Hellenistic and the Late Roman, we found more or less indisputable evidence that pottery was actually being made here, in the form of "kiln-wasters"—that is, pieces of vessels that were misfired in the kiln and then discarded. Along the southern perimeter, there are also visible what may be the traces of a fortification wall. The area of the site fills most of the dip between the two hills, far left and center in Figure 31.

Another argument that seems to us very persuasive from the point of view of the identification of the site arises from a piece of evidence that has been known for over 120 years, and has not prevented some scholars from looking for the site of Askra some

8. W. M. Leake, *Travels in Northern Greece*, vol. 2 (1835), 492–93.

miles away. A bare kilometer to the west of the edge of our large
site, there lies a much smaller one ("Valley of the Muses 27"),
occupied at some of the same periods and marked, at a much
later date, by a chapel of Agios Loukas. Here in 1860, in or beside the then still standing chapel, was found part of a Roman
inscription, the epitaph for a young girl (*IG* 7. 1883), the closing
lines of which (*IG* 7. 1884) had been discovered even earlier at
the same spot.[9] A poem in elegiac couplets is put in the mouth of
the dead girl, and the now completed text included the phrase
"The Askraian plain covers me." This is, of course, a poetic
expression, but it seems perverse to take the words in any sense
other than that this district, at least in the later Roman period,
went by the name of Askra—especially now that we know that
the find spot is a genuine ancient site, perhaps an outlying grave-
yard for the main town nearby.

Our site, therefore, seems almost certainly to be that of Askra,
the village to which Hesiod tells us his father migrated from Ionia
(*Works and Days* 639–40). It has become common in recent
years, and justifiably so, for critics to look askance at what pur-
port to be autobiographical passages in the early Greek poets.[10]
In this case, we can at least say that the association between Hesiod and Askra had become established fairly soon after the
poet's lifetime, for Plutarch (*Moralia* fr. 82) tells us, attributing
the information to Aristotle, that on one occasion the inhabitants
of Askra fled to Orchomenos, taking with them the bones of Hesiod, which had originally been buried elsewhere but later repa-
triated to Askra. This episode thus cannot be dated later than the
lifetime of Aristotle, and the reburial of the bones must, of
course, have been earlier still. The chronology of our site shows

9. See A. M. Snodgrass, "The Site of Askra," in *La Béotie antique* (Col-
loques internationaux du CNRS), ed. G. Argoud and P. Roesch (Lyon, 1985),
87–95.

10. See, for example, M. Griffith, "Personality in Hesiod," *Classical Antiquity* 2 (1983): 37–65.

that, if it was Askra, then it was already an established place by the time Hesiod's father came (in the eighth century B.C.). The evidence also implies that, at least in later periods, it became a substantial enough place to manufacture its own pottery—incidentally recalling another Hesiodic phrase, "Potter begrudges potter" (*Works and Days* 25); and in general it offers a plausible setting for those passages in the *Works and Days* that suggest that their author lived in, or at least frequented, a sizeable village (e.g., 343–47, 493–94). The site shows a period of apparent desertion just when Pausanias says that Askra was deserted, and it is dominated by a tower that conforms well enough to Pausanias's reference to the tower, in the general vicinity of Mount Helikon, that marked Askra. Its location, in the midst of a sea of vineyards, even throws some dim light on a passage of Strabo (9. 2.35): the geographer, discussing a variant reading in the Homeric Catalogue of Ships, "Askra rich in vines," is trapped by his reliance on secondhand evidence into the mistaken view that this would give the place an inappropriate epithet. In fact, firsthand familiarity with the district, and even perhaps with the text of the *Works and Days* (especially 609–14), might have given him a better basis on which to found his opinions. One thing that we have conspicuously failed to do is to account for Hesiod's disparagement of his family's adoptive home (*Works and Days* 639–40): certainly Askra, like many places at nearly 1,500 feet above sea level, does not have a gentle winter climate; but his next phrase, *therei argaleēi*, often translated "sultry in summer," and certainly pejorative in general sense, remains entirely obscure to us and may tell more about Hesiod (or about his chosen persona) than about Askra.

In this selection from the findings of our survey, I have passed over many important matters, both of detail and of principle; but it may give a preliminary basis on which to assess the whole method of archaeological survey and its potential contribution. Survey is sometimes dismissed as an activity essentially both an-

cillary to excavation, and parasitic upon it. How far can our findings stand without the excavation of one or more of our "sites,"
in order to test our interpretation of them—particularly that of
the numerous isolated rural "farmsteads"? How could we begin
to determine their chronology, were it not for a century or more
of prior excavation work that has established the dating of the
Greek pottery styles? Would we not in fact have discovered much
more of value had we spent the past five seasons excavating a
single Boeotian site?

Let me try to offer some sort of answer, beginning with this
last question. If we had indeed been excavating, say, a rural settlement for five years, we should have discovered more and
better-preserved finds; of that there is little doubt. But would this
material have told us anything about anywhere beyond the site
itself, in return for the greater demands that it would have made
on the precious space in Thebes Museum? The notion that the
excavation of a single site will convey information about the region of which that site formed the center is widespread among
archaeologists, as countless statements in their writings show; in
many cases, its status is that of an unspoken assumption. The
more important the site, the larger the area over which it is likely
to have exercised control, and of which therefore its finds are usually taken to be representative. Yet how valid is this whole notion? I would venture to suggest that it is really a kind of archaeological convention: a device of convenience, adopted in tacit
recognition of the fact that it is not normally possible to excavate
even a representative sample of the region, let alone the region en
bloc. If the chosen site was in some sense the *political* capital of
a block of territory, however small, then of course the claim of
the finds to speak for that territory is slightly reinforced, but even
then the scope of the representation is strictly limited. The reality
of excavation, which is also very seldom explicitly recognized, is
that few sites will in any case be uncovered in their entirety; as
we saw from the examples quoted at the end of chapter 2, exca-

vation resembles survey in that it habitually involves processes of sampling, and of extrapolating from the investigated fraction to the whole unit. The main difference between the two is perhaps that, when the unit is a site under excavation, the choice of that sample is more likely to be constrained by fortuitous external factors, such as the position of modern buildings or the availability of land for purchase.[11]

By contrast our findings, if they tell us anything, are telling us about a region: arguably, if the sample has been well or fortunately chosen, quite a sizeable region of Boeotia; but if not, then just the smaller area that has actually been surveyed. This is a stretch of land in which, at times, a number of people may have lived, and in which, beyond doubt, a very much larger number of people obtained their main livelihood, over very long periods. A density map of the finds observed over one part of that area, like Figure 30, is conveying a body of evidence that can be checked and reinvestigated at the most fundamental level, as well as reinterpreted or merely extended.

It is also a body of evidence that one can hardly imagine being assembled through excavation—which brings us to another of the questions posed just now, about the need for validating our conclusions by means of test-excavation of one or more of our sites. A persuasive case could be made for just such a procedure. The careful and total excavation of just one "farmstead" site would, for instance, be invaluable as a test of how far the significant periods of occupation coincided with those conspicuously represented in the surface finds. But as a test of our interpretation of the function of the whole class of such sites, it would be less decisive: the process would really need to be extended over a

11. These and other issues have been aired by J. F. Cherry in "Frogs Round the Pond: Perspectives on Current Archaeological Survey Projects in the Mediterranean Region," in *Archaeological Survey in the Mediterranean Area*, British Archaeological Reports, International Series, no. 155, ed. D. W. Rupp and D. Keller (Oxford, 1983), 375–416, and in his subsequent exchanges with R. Hope Simpson in *JFA* 11 (1984): 115–20.

larger number of sites that were similar in respect of their surface
traces. Even then, it would by no means follow that the issues left
in doubt by the survey would be settled by the excavation. The
distinction between seasonal and permanent human occupation,
after all, is one that requires some sophistication in the analysis
even of excavation finds. At all events our present intention,
though posterity may judge it to be misguided, is to see how far
knowledge can be advanced by surface study alone. Though we
admit the likelihood that excavation would add a degree of cer-
titude to our findings, we are even more aware of the need for
survey to prove itself, at least in the classical context, as a viable
branch of independent research.

The charge of parasitism is indeed directly raised by the remaining question asked just now: are we not entirely dependent
on earlier excavation work for the whole chronological system
within which we operate? Here again, there is no harm in frankly
admitting our debt; but it is a debt to the entire range of existing
archaeological studies. The dating of the Greek pottery styles,
as a matter of historical fact, has been established as much, or
more, by stylistic analysis as by stratified excavation finds. At
some points, indeed, excavators may find themselves as dependent on this rich seam of traditional research in classical archaeology as surveyors. All our efforts should ideally be seen as
complementary.

I have argued in this chapter that, in the task of understanding
and explaining the classical past, survey offers an entirely fresh
and potentially valuable dimension. It is a dimension that brings
out very clearly another relationship, emphasized in some recent
nonclassical work, but previously much neglected: I mean the relationship of the archaeological record to the present day. "The
archaeological record," writes Lewis Binford, "is here with us in
the present. . . . and the observations we make about it are in the

here and now"; they are "not 'historical' statements."[12] The truth of this observation is perhaps more apparent to the surveyor, painfully conscious of the vulnerability of his raw data to the effects of seasonal, even ephemeral, modern activity, than it is to the excavator; for we all share to some degree the illusion that a progress downwards into the earth is a journey backwards into the past. It is not: the stratified deposits uncovered by the excavator all began their existence as surface deposits, for however fleeting a period, and were thus subject to some of the processes of degradation, displacement, and dispersal for which the data of surface survey are often criticized; not to mention the multifarious effects of "post-depositional" factors once these deposits disappeared from sight. There is perhaps a certain monitory value in a method that starkly exhibits these limitations.

In our particular case, the contribution that we believe ourselves to be making to the history of Boeotia is certainly not to a history conceived in traditional terms; but it is to a kind of history that more and more historians today are accepting as a worthwhile aim. In particular, to recover any small part of the history of the rural landscape of ancient Greece will be to break almost entirely new ground—as well as giving new force to the inscription on Hilgard Hall.

12. L. R. Binford, *In Pursuit of the Past* (London, 1983), 19, 23.

CHAPTER FIVE

The First Figure-scenes in Greek Art

The change of subject at this juncture may seem abrupt; but there is an underlying unity of theme behind the disparity of subject matter. Classical archaeology has been criticized within the archaeological world for its isolation from the mainstream of archaeological research, yet in my view it is placed to reenter that common tradition from a position of strength. Similarly, classical archaeology stands accused of applying outmoded methods in art history, yet here, too, as I hope we shall see, it can offer something distinctive to the field as a whole. In terms of sheer quantity, the volume of past work in ancient art history is so huge that to omit the study of Greek art from an investigation of Greek archaeology would either show an absurd lack of proportion or, if done as an act of policy, be an example of precisely the kind of doctrinaire compartmentalization that I have been deploring. It seems to me a strength, not a weakness, of classical archaeology that it should automatically be taken to include the study of art, and that the same people should often choose to practice, and be required to teach, in both fields. The special contribution the subject can make to art history derives from this very circumstance, that the same people can be expected both to offer the artistic analysis *and* to have mastered the archaeological evidence.

Judged by its own standards, the past tradition of study of classical art, in addition to its volume and duration, has been distinguished. Yet criticisms of it cannot, and should not, be silenced. Let me quote one of them, which is so comprehensive that it can perhaps do duty for a whole range of more specific charges. It is the statement made in 1966 by Ranuccio Bianchi Bandinelli, a distinguished exponent of the subject himself, that classical archaeology is guilty of "the almost total abandonment of art history."[1] This is the sort of charge that may tempt the classical archaeologist, as his wife exhorted Job, to curse God and die. The vast investment of time and scholarship in the study of Greek and Roman art has shown no sign of diminishing, let alone coming to an end, in recent years; its scale and preponderance within the discipline are intermittently a subject for disparagement among the latter's critics; if, after all that expenditure of effort, the result cannot even be dignified by the name of art history, then what purpose has it served? It will help if I clarify a little the context of Bianchi Bandinelli's comment: he was attacking what he felt to be the obsession with classification and dating, and the search for parallels and attributions, pursued by classical archaeologists to the neglect, often the exclusion, of true art history. To this, his numerous opponents would at once have replied that such classificatory work is an absolutely indispensable first step in a field such as classical art, which is relatively ill-documented by the standards of later art history, before anything in the nature of critical interpretation can be attempted. But the point of the criticism is that this "preliminary" work, on its own, seems to exhaust the time, the scholarship, and apparently the interest of the classical art historian. One may venture to suggest, again, that

1. R. Bianchi Bandinelli, "Quelques réflexions à propos des rapports entre archéologie et histoire de l'art," in *Mélanges offerts à Kazimierz Michalowski* (Warsaw, 1966), 262. For a parallel opinion about the study of Greek vases in the past century, see H. Hoffman, "In the Wake of Beazley," *Hephaistos* 1 (1979): 61–70, especially 61 on "the virtual exclusion of inquiries concerned with the meaning, function and cultural relevance of these objects."

psychological factors are at work: the appeal of this kind of study to the convergent intellect, with its appetite for the single, right answer, will be apparent.

Another kind of rejoinder might today be given to Bianchi Bandinelli's charge: that, in the fairly short time since he brought it, classical archaeologists have discernibly mended their ways; that true classical art history is now alive and well, practiced indeed by several dissident schools simultaneously. One symptom of this revival might be that discussion of an art-historical problem of especial importance to Greek art has come vigorously to life after some two generations of relative neglect. The problem is that of the relationship between narrative and artistic representation. There are several reasons why this question is central to Greek art; two of them may be illustrated by two of the more emphatic claims that have been made for Greek artists in this field. First, John Carter's proposition, in the course of a valuable article on the subject in 1972, that the Greeks virtually invented narrative art;[2] second, Gombrich's well-known argument that what lay behind the historic appearance of naturalism in Greek art was "the character of Greek narration": that a special gift or quality, hitherto revealed mainly in the literary medium, inspired the sculptors and painters of Greece to create the achievement Gombrich called "The Greek Revolution."[3]

It was this theory of Gombrich's that Carter used in discussing his own material, notwithstanding that he himself was writing mainly about Geometric art of the eighth century B.C., whereas Gombrich's "Greek Revolution" was something that he explicitly dated between the limits of about 550 and 400 B.C. Both writers are clearly impressed (as innumerable others have been) by the frequency in Greek art of scenes with a narrative content, and by the fact that, in the majority of these scenes, that content is spe-

2. J. Carter, "The Beginning of Narrative Art in the Greek Geometric Period," *BSA* 67 (1972): 25–58, especially 26.
3. E. H. Gombrich, *Art and Illusion* (Oxford, 1960), 110; cf. 99.

cifically mythical or legendary. As always in this field, one has to be very careful about one's terminology: it would be possible, for example, to define "narrative" either in a sense so narrow that it would greatly reduce the body of material open to discussion; or in a sense so wide as to make it a false claim that myth and legend preponderate, as I have said that they do. As a matter of fact, today one has to be careful about a great deal more than one's terminology; for we must reckon with new interpretations of these same phenomena, which not only differ from, but may even entirely exclude the approach we have begun to consider.

The Structuralist interpretation comes under this heading. Anyone familiar with the Structuralist view of myth—that a given myth is made up of all its variants, that the narrative sequence and content of all or any of these variants is unimportant, and that what matters is the *structure* of the myth, reflecting as it does the structure of the human mind—and more especially, anyone who has read the remarkable sentences in Lévi-Strauss's retrospective survey of his own work on myth, about the study of myth making possible a "conspiracy against time," even the "abolition of time"[4]—may not be surprised at what is coming next. It is clear that such a doctrine of myth will have some repercussions on one's view of mythical narrative *in art*. If time and temporal sequence are peripheral to the nature of a myth, then they are not likely to be judged important ingredients of a myth-picture. But where will this leave the wide range of scholarly work that has been devoted to the treatment of temporal sequence in Greco-Roman art? Such work has taken as its first field our richest corpus of evidence, Greek vase-paintings; and, as I have already hinted, it has been notably concentrated in two periods, the generation after the appearance of Carl Robert's *Bild und Lied* in 1881, and our own generation. One strand of this investigation has been focused on that interesting device,

4. C. Lévi-Strauss, *L'Homme nu* (Mythologiques 4) (Paris, 1971), especially 542.

adopted by some Archaic vase-painters, whereby a single picture combines a series of episodes in a story as if they were simultaneous, but—a very important restriction—without allowing any single figure to appear in the picture more than once.[5]

This practice has, at different periods, been called the "complementary" (*komplettierend*), "simultaneous," or "synoptic" method. One of the more interesting results of the study of this method has been the revelation that such a way of conceiving a myth in visual terms was, at least as far as Greece was concerned, the original innovation of Archaic artists (and quite possibly of vase-painters specifically). It is significant that the examples of Aegean Bronze Age art in which the treatment of successive episodes of a story has been detected—for instance, in fresco and inlay work,[6] and in the series of gold rings discussed in the 1941 Sather Lectures of Axel Persson[7]—have all been claimed to represent a quite different method or methods, in which either the principal figure (or figures) are repeated in order to show the passage of time, *or* the same end is achieved by showing a row of different figures in the postures that would be successively occupied by one figure as time passed.

This technique, even if correctly diagnosed, is uncommon in later Greek art; whereas the "simultaneous" or "synoptic" method is, for a time, characteristic of it. The classic illustration, which I apologize for showing yet again, is an Attic black-figure cup of about 550 B.C. in Boston that portrays the story, familiar from the tenth book of the *Odyssey*, of Circe's transformation of

5. See my *Narration and Allusion in Archaic Greek Art* (11th Myres Memorial Lecture, Oxford, 1982) in a somewhat oversimplified form.

6. See J. L. Myres, "Homeric art," *BSA* 45 (1950): 233, on the "Taureador fresco" as showing the successive positions of a single acrobat (cf. A. J. Evans, *The Palace of Minos*, vol. 3 [London, 1930], 223, fig. 156); and compare Myres, 245, on the "Lion hunt dagger-blade," showing "phases through which any one warrior may pass."

7. A. W. Persson, *The Religion of Greece in Prehistoric Times*, Sather Classical Lectures, no. 17 (Berkeley, 1942), 28–30, 47, 80–81. Figures 49 and 50 in this volume illustrate two of these.

Figure 35. Attic black-figure cup (Boston), with scene of Circe and Odysseus's sailors.

Odysseus's sailors (Figure 35).[8] The picture, in some respects very faithful to the Homeric account, shows Circe mixing the potion that will transform the sailors into animals, that will lead the suspicious Eurylochos to steal off and give the alarm, that will provoke Odysseus to come and threaten Circe into reversing the spell—yet all these three subsequent episodes are already shown taking place (right and left of center, far right, and far left respectively). To the layman, "synoptic" pictures of this kind seem to represent time defied; to the Structuralist, they show something rather different (and more "Structuralist"): time disregarded.

In presuming to represent their view here, I am in something of an embarrassment. Lévi-Strauss himself has written extensively about art, but his well-known predilection for studying "cold," as opposed to "hot," or historically documented, cultures means that there is no treatment by him of the kind of work that we are looking at here. Nor have I even been able to find specific statement of the doctrine in question in the writings of the "Paris School" of classicists, who under the recent leadership of Jean-Pierre Vernant have turned their attention to many such prob-

8. Cup, Boston 99.518; J. D. Beazley, *ABV* 198.

lems. The truth is that I am relying on oral expositions, given by
adherents of the Paris School who are also in sympathy with
Structuralism; and if I am doing less than justice to a view I actually find very persuasive, then I trust that matters will shortly
be set to rights in print. The central assumption of the argument,
as I understand it, is that the whole notion of "time" in the context of such works, as employed for instance in my description
of the Circe picture just given, is an anachronistic modern im-
portation; that the artist himself was not conscious of it, and
therefore equally unconscious that he was, to the literal-minded
spectator, defying it. All that he meant to show, by portraying
different characters involved in different actions that, in the
story, took place at different times, was merely the distinctive and
characteristic attribute of each figure. Circe *is* the sorceress, the
sailors *are* the victims and so on, and each must therefore be
given his or her essential action or attribute; the inherent structure of the myth, which is thereby portrayed, is a timeless one.
Any apparent violation of time was thus an accidental by-
product of the artist's concern with another, to him more important, question. A possible implication is that much the same was
true of later artists who intermittently handled similar themes in
a similar way, right down to the invention of photography, which
is mainly responsible for alerting man's sensitivity to these apparent "violations" of the unity of time. If it is true that the producers of such scenes and their publics wished only to see each
character given his or her individual action or epithet, then this
will deny to such pictures the strict status of "narrative art"; indeed the doctrine could be pursued to the point of denying the
possibility of true narrative art at all.

Let me at once admit that this theory, when applied to a number of works of Greek art, gives convincing results. It can equally
well be applied to another, quite separate, category of ancient
pictures that are *non*-episodic: that is to say, that appear to respect unity of time by showing only actions that happened, or
could have happened, at the same moment in a given sequence

of episodes. These pictures are less frequent, or less conspicuous, in Archaic Greek art, but they become almost the norm in the full Classical period, when the passion for presenting eventful legendary tales in their full detail had somewhat waned. Here, the Structuralist explanation will be that the apparent "unity of time" is but a coincidence: the characteristic actions or epithets given to each figure happened, in this case, to be compatible with one another in temporal terms, according to the accepted version of the story. Only if we can detect independent signs of a concern with temporal issues on the artist's part—and this we are much more likely to be able to do with the first, "synoptic" type of picture than with the second kind just described—are we entitled to contest an interpretation that conforms as well as this to what we can actually observe. I wish now to draw attention to a few cases where I think we *can* detect such signs; but I should say, in anticipation of the main argument of this chapter, that for some purposes this apparent polarity of views need not be resolved, but can be by-passed. Whether we believe that the Archaic artists were defying time or merely ignoring it, the end-product of their endeavors remains unchanged, and this end-product is susceptible of other kinds of analysis in which the question of the thought-processes of the artist is not a crucial one.

We have already referred to several different ways in which ancient artists, at least on a naive reading, appear to have set about "telling a story" in visual terms: by compressing several successive episodes into a single moment; by choosing a single moment in the first place; or, in the Bronze Age, by showing successive episodes *as* successive through repetition or multiplication of figures. At the risk of complicating things still further, I should mention here yet another method that is sometimes used. This involves representing a *series* of exploits of one heroic figure, with a separate panel or picture being devoted to each exploit; in this case, of course, the hero reappears in each scene. The prime medium for this treatment is architectural relief-sculpture, but it also appears, slightly adapted, in a group of vase-paintings that

show some of the deeds of Theseus. It has been noticed, for example, that in the twelve sculptured metopes of the Temple of
Zeus at Olympia that portray the twelve labors of Herakles, or
in the group of Attic red-figure vases just mentioned that illustrate Theseus's exploits, the artists do not respect the "official"
temporal sequence in which the deeds were supposed to have
been performed, but instead allow themselves either to rearrange
the order to suit their artistic purpose or to omit episodes no less
important than the ones they show.[9] This shows that there were
at least some contexts in which time was, to say the least, not an
ever-present subject of concern—just as the Structuralist view
would lead us to expect.

The real test for the validity of that view comes, however, in
the context of the "synoptic" pictures with which we began.
Whereas in the case of the "separate panel" treatment, it is only
the moderately well informed spectator (ancient or modern) who
will be aware that there is any violation of the accepted time-se-
quence, with the "synoptic" treatment it is temporal *logic* that
appears to be infringed, and certainly any modern viewer who
stops to analyze the picture for a minute or two will become
aware of that violation. The question that faces us is whether the
artist himself, and his contemporary public, were conscious of
any such thing. Let us use the Structuralist language of "attributes" or "epithets" in approaching one instance that is representative of a larger group of pictures: those in which a single figure
is given more than one "attribute." On a Lakonian black-figure
cup, once again of about 550 B.C., we see one of the more elab-
orate vase-pictures of the story of the blinding of Polyphemos
(Figure 36).[10] We are shown the Cyclops devouring the limbs of

9. Compare V. Dasen, "Autour du dinos de Néarchos: Essai sur la bande
dessinée chez les anciens," *Etudes de Lettres* (1983), pt. 4, 55–73, especially
64–65.

10. Cup, Paris, Cabinet de Médailles 190; C. M. Stibbe, *Lakonische Vasen-
maler des sechsten Jahrhunderts v. Chr.* (Amsterdam and London, 1972), 285,
no. 289.

Figure 36. Lakonian black-figure cup (Paris, Bibliothèque Nationale), with scene of Polyphemos and Odysseus.

Odysseus's sailors, while about to drink from the cup that will induce the drunkenness that will cause him to fall into the sleep that will enable Odysseus and his surviving comrades to blind him—as they are also shown doing. On the traditional analysis, which we used in first approaching the Circe cup, the artist has here compressed three of the five successive episodes just listed into a single moment. For the Structuralist, all that he has done is to give two "epithets" (roughly speaking, cannibalism and drunkenness) to Polyphemos, and another (the stake for the blinding) to Odysseus and his companions.

We may wish to protest here that the temporal "collision" is too obvious for anybody to miss; but in saying this we may be merely revealing our anachronistic prejudices. A better approach may be to pose a question: Polyphemos may be "the cannibal," "the drunkard," *and* "the victim"; but can he be all three simultaneously and (more important) *inherently*? Are all three features essential components of the structure of the myth? A detailed analysis of the numerous variants of this story by Claude Calame suggests otherwise. The act of cannibalism, he suggests, and the act of retribution that avenges it, the blinding, are balancing and critically important features of any version of the story. By contrast, the role played by the cup of wine is not so obviously essential to the structure; Polyphemos (with his non-Greek counterparts) is not "always" the drunkard, either in the sense that this detail is present in all versions, or in the more trivial sense that, in the Greek version, he is "always" drinking (on the contrary, in Homer Odysseus's wine is a special treat for him). In this case, therefore, one might ask which is the more likely explanation: that the painter included all the attributes that he felt essential to the characterization of his figures; or that, having decided to show the cannibalism and the blinding, he felt that the transition between the two would be too abrupt unless he inserted an intermediate temporal stage in the form of the cup (at the cost of some awkwardness, since Polyphemos has no free hand with which to hold it).[11]

There may still be difficulty in making a choice between the alternatives, so I shall turn to another, slightly later picture in which this same element of "multiple epithets" applied to a single figure is present, together with other, rarer features. It is the scene running continuously round the shoulder of an Attic black-figure hydria by the Antimenes Painter (about 520 B.C.), and it is one of the most arresting new works of Greek vase-painting to come

11. See C. Calame, "La Légende du Cyclops dans le folklore européen et extra-européen: Un Jeu de transformations narratives," *Etudes de Lettres* (1977), pt. 2, 45–79, especially 64.

Figures 37, 38. Two views of the scene on the shoulder of an Attic black-figure hydria (Basel, private collection), with scene of Neoptolemos at Troy.

to light in recent years (Figures 37–38).[12] The subject is generically common but individually very rare: the *aristeia,* or prowess in battle, of Neoptolemos at Troy, which was treated in the lost epic called the *Little Iliad.* From the right (at first sight surprisingly, since the left is the "winner's side" in Attic vase-painting), Athena runs up to support her protégé Neoptolemos, whose chariot follows next to the left; to the left again, we see, first the hero's handiwork, the corpse of his most noted opponent, the Trojan ally Eurypylos, with one of Neoptolemos's spears still fixed in his body, and with his armor already stripped off him by his conqueror. This was Neoptolemos's hardest victory, singled out for mention by Odysseus when he tries to cheer the ghost of Achilles by regaling him with his son's more recent exploits (*Odyssey* 11. 520). To the left again, we at last see Neoptolemos himself, on foot, in the very act of spearing in the back a fleeing charioteer, who cries out and throws back his head in agony. Whose charioteer this is is not absolutely clear, because next to the left again we find another fallen enemy, Helikaon, whom we know to have been the son of the Trojan Antenor, but whom we did *not* know to have been killed at Troy, by Neoptolemos or anyone else: indeed we hear from Pausanias of an incident in the epic cycle when his life was spared by Odysseus after he was wounded, and from Martial that he escaped after the fall of Troy and became one of the founders of Patavium in northern Italy. In this picture, however, as Mark Davies has pointed out, the signs are that Helikaon is dead.[13] Finally, at the far left and *from* the left, Apollo advances brandishing his bow to put a stop at last to

12. For knowledge of this scene, painted on the shoulder of a still unpublished hydria in Basel, I depend on the photographs in K. Schefold, *Götter- und Heldensagen der Griechen in der spätarchaischen Kunst* (Munich, 1978), figs. 339–40, and on the comments of the scholars mentioned in the next footnote.

13. See M. I. Davies, "The Reclamation of Helen," *Ant.K.* 20 (1977): 75 n. 12; cf. also the views of J. D. Beazley, *Paralipomena* (Oxford, 1971), 119–20, no. 35 *bis.* The interpretations do not coincide with those of Schefold's text and captions (cited above, n. 12), 252–54 in all particulars—for example as to the exact role of Apollo or the attribution of chariots to warriors.

Neoptolemos's triumphant progress; thus we find the explanation for the fact that the hero's direction of progress has been from right to left—in the last resort he will *not* conquer. Apollo, the protector of Troy, will stop him from taking the city (just as he stopped his father in similar circumstances at the end of book 21 of the *Iliad*).

Two things about this picture suggest to me that the painter has handled the dimension of time with conscious deliberation. First, the killing of the charioteer is an instantaneous representation of the moment of death, set in the middle of a sequence of three killings. Second, the temporal sequence unrolls from right to left, and has to occupy an appreciable length of time. Neoptolemos has had time not only to spear Eurypylos, but to strip him of his armor. Epic heroes use two spears, and it is with his second one that Neoptolemos is just now killing the charioteer; he must, however, retain this one in order to encompass the death of Helikaon, in whose body a spear (presumably this same one) is again fixed. Finally, Neoptolemos will be halted by Apollo. That this is the sequence of events is confirmed by a partial duplicate of this scene by the same painter: on another hydria, in Würzburg,[14] an almost identical Neoptolemos is spearing an almost identical charioteer, while the presumed Helikaon, wounded but still alive, crawls vainly in the direction of his doomed chariot and driver. Thus, the death of Helikaon should be set in the future relative to that of the driver. The temporal sequence runs consistently from right to left. On the Structuralist view, this becomes something of a coincidence: the artist wished only to portray Neoptolemos's prowess by giving him three victims, and just happened to arrange the three, plus the fourth and final episode with Apollo, in a right-to-left order. The last point, together with the observation about the spears, and the central emphasis on the moment of the charioteer's death, seem all to tell in favor of the other interpretation—*in this case*. But it would still be open to

14. Hydria, Würzburg 309: *ABV* 268, no. 28.

the Structuralist to respond that this is a very unusual vase-painting: we are not used to seeing a single instant in a narrative sequence given this dramatic emphasis in Archaic Greek art.

The most that I have succeeded in showing is that some artists, sometimes, look as though they were conscious of the fact that, in using the "synoptic" method of presenting a story, they had to manipulate time. This point may perhaps be reinforced by one last example, taken from the much smaller group of works in which the chosen subject matter was taken not from legend but from history. In his description of the mural of the Battle of Marathon in the Stoa Poikilē at Athens, Pausanias (1. 15.4) says that "at the beginning" the two sides were shown coming to grips; "things are about evenly balanced. But in the heart of the battle the barbarians are in flight . . . and the painting comes to an end at the Phoenician ships." Presumably, the direction of the sequence from the "beginning" to the "end" was left-to-right; but irrespective of this, it is clear from Pausanias's description that he could understand the time-dimension as running from one side to the other, and the painter must have intended him to do so. We may also note a telling feature of the description: the leading figures on the battlefield, of whom there were several, were evidently shown only once each—exactly as we have found to be the rule in the "synoptic" vase-paintings. The conclusion seems clear that an artist, working in this much grander medium, still felt constrained to observe the rules of a "synoptic" representation; and that his subject, which required him to present a fairly recent historical event in circumstantial and more or less accurate detail, also compelled him to use the time-dimension clearly and consciously.

Whether or not the examples that I have given prove to be representative of all Archaic Greek art, the fact remains that in all genuine uses of the "synoptic" method, unity of time is not present: the statement remains empirically true even if it is merely a statement of modern descriptive attitude. This is the point to be borne in mind as we turn our search backwards in time in an attempt to seek out the origins of this artistic method. For this, I think we have to go back to a date some two centuries earlier than that of the three black-figure vases that we have looked at—that is, to the time of the first massed figures in surviving Greek art, on the vases of the Late Geometric style. The interpretation of these scenes has formed the subject of intense discussion in recent years, but it remains one of the unresolved disputes of classical art history. This very fact, that the deployment of traditional approaches has resulted not in a consensus but in a stalemate, is part of my reason for choosing it as the main theme of this chapter. Can we make use of the circumstance mentioned earlier—that the handling of the archaeological context of these Geometric vases, and the interpretation of the scenes on them, rest with the same group of people—to start building a truly integrated analysis of them?

First, I recapitulate the current state of the debate over the interpretation of the Geometric scenes. Each of the two main schools of thought—those who see in these pictures the evocation of a heroic past, and those who read them as portrayals of contemporary life—bases its arguments partly on analogy with literature and with Greek art of the ensuing period that is better understood, but ultimately, on an appeal to common sense credibility. Each, as a consequence, seems to find in the other's conclusions a violation of such credibility. Attempts to find a mediating, compromise solution, either on a simple level (that some of the scenes are heroic, some from real life), or on a more sophisticated one (that, from the moment of their creation, the scenes were meant to be ambivalent) seem destined for rejection by both sides, as is often the fate of the peacemaker's efforts.[15] If there is any way of establishing a common ground of objective

---

15. See most recently J. Boardman, "Symbol and Story in Geometric Art," in *Ancient Greek Art and Iconography*, ed. W. Moon (Madison, Wis., 1983), 15–36, who rejects compromises such as those proposed by Isler and Kannicht (cited below, n. 24).

observation and verifiable hypothesis, then this should be done without further delay.

Let us begin with a statement about the context of these pictures that at least has the merit of being quantitative. Large crowd scenes with massed figures are, in Geometric art, confined to funerary vases, many of them apparently markers that stood over graves, visible to the passerby. Two subjects predominate: the *prothesis*, or lying in state of a corpse before its burial (Figure 39), and the battle scene, whether on land, on sea, or amphibious (Figure 40). Both subjects have been treated in valuable monographs by Gudrun Ahlberg, and from her catalogues we learn that fifty out of fifty-two *prothesis* scenes known in 1971 were Attic, and twenty-six out of twenty-eight battle scenes: 96 and 93 percent respectively. Moreover, their scope is not only restricted geographically, but heavily concentrated in time: as Ahlberg observes in her book on the battle scenes, the great majority of them (sixteen out of the twenty-two that are readily datable) come from a single Athenian workshop whose activity may have lasted little more than a decade, around 750 B.C. on the conventional dating.[16] We are looking, in other words, at the work of a tiny group of craftsmen, over a short space of time, in a single location. With the *prothesis* scenes, the time-span is longer and the diversity of style, partly but not entirely because of this, greater; yet the range of *composition* is, if anything, rather narrower than with the battle scenes—the essential formula for a *prothesis* on Attic vases, once established, changed little over the two generations of its prevalence.

So much for the producers; what of their customers? Another striking feature of the Late Geometric crowd scenes is that the great majority of them have been known, or at least in existence

16. G. Ahlberg, *Prothesis and Ekphora in Greek Geometric Art*, Studies in Mediterranean Archaeology, no. 32 (Göteborg, 1971), and *Fighting on Land and Sea in Greek Geometric Art*, Skrifter utgivna av Svenska Institutet i Athen, no. 16 (Stockholm, 1971). For questions of production, provenance, and date, see Ahlberg's catalogues in *Prothesis and Ekphora*, 23–29, with references, and cf. 281 for comment; and in *Fighting on Land and Sea*, 12, 25–26 with references, 39–41, 66.

Figure 39. Fragment of Attic Geometric krater (Paris, Louvre A 517).

Figure 40. Fragment of Attic Geometric krater (Paris, Louvre A 519).

above ground, for about a hundred years. More recent additions to their number have come in a very slow trickle, and consist mainly of relatively late and simplified *prothesis* scenes. The bulk of the battle scenes—again, about three-quarters—can be shown, or strongly suspected, to have been found in the excavation of a series of rich graves on the modern Piraeus Street in Athens in the last thirty years of the nineteenth century, where they often featured (as in Figures 39 and 40) on vases erected as markers. Even though the pieces have become scattered among a number of museums in several countries, their essential unity was demonstrated some years ago when scholars found that fragments in different collections actually joined.[17] This observation strongly reinforces our previous one about the concentration in time of the battle scenes: most of these pictures were produced not only by, but also for, a handful of people—the family group or groups that used the Piraeus Street cemetery. The elusiveness of closely comparable pottery in the hundreds of Athenian graves of similar period excavated in more recent years gives a powerful hint of the exclusiveness, in both social and local terms, of the group that bought, and possibly commissioned, these vases.

All of this acts as a deterrent, in at least two ways, to any attempt at unraveling the meaning of the scenes on the vases. First, the group for which they were destined may have been utterly unrepresentative of contemporary society in Athens, let alone the wider Greek world; so that inferences drawn from what we know from other sources of beliefs and practices among the Greeks at this time, and from what we see on other contemporary art, may be misleading. Ideally, such inferences should be derived from the associations and burial circumstances of these same few graves; but unfortunately, because of the very early date of their discovery, this information is mostly lost for ever. The second deterrent is that we cannot necessarily expect the fu-

17. Cf. J. N. Coldstream, *Greek Geometric Pottery* (London, 1968), 29–33, with references to the earlier work of E. Kunze (1953) and F. Villard (1949 and 1954).

ture to bring substantial additions to the body of evidence; we cannot therefore form hypotheses and see them verified or falsified by later finds, in the way that archaeologists often can. Our interpretations must therefore be based on a body of data that may be too small for a convincing, let alone "conclusive," statement, in terms of probabilities, to be made about them.

I shall nevertheless venture on a statistical observation about the battle scenes, which arises from a remark made in a review of Ahlberg's *Fighting on Land and Sea in Greek Geometric Art* a decade ago by Nicolas Coldstream.[18] It concerns a particular bone of contention in the controversy about the meaning of the Geometric scenes: the "Dipylon shield" carried by so many of the warrior figures in them. I am not going to reopen the old controversy as to whether or not these shields can be taken as a sign that the artist is giving his picture a heroic setting. Instead, I wish to use as a statistical unit the individual figure, rather than as hitherto the complete scene. We have some twenty-three figures of warriors holding these shields, or else of isolated shields without a user, shown in actual combat scenes, as opposed to pictures of people marching, parading, or standing by.[19] Of these twenty-three, some seven are either insufficiently well preserved for it to be clear what will be the outcome, or are shown at a point where the fighting has not yet reached a decisive stage. This leaves a residue of sixteen where the warrior is in the thick of battle; and of these, every single one looks like losing. Four are dead or at the point of death (as in Figure 40, top right); two others are already pierced by weapons; four are being disarmed, apparently after capture, and so probably is a fifth, on another vase, who has dropped his shield and is leaning over backwards; two must be listed as "missing, presumed killed," since their shields are shown

18. *Gnomon* 46 (1974): 395.
19. All these scenes are conveniently illustrated in Ahlberg's *Fighting on Land and Sea* (cited above, n. 16); for one or two details that are difficult to make out, I rely on her descriptive comments.

Figure 41. Attic Geometric oenochoë (Copenhagen),
with scene of land and sea battle.

being carried off on the deck of a departing warship, presumably
as booty; while the remaining three (two of them shown in Figure
41) are still embattled, in circumstances where it appears that
their comrades are dead or wounded, and there is little evidence
of damage to their enemies.

Now sixteen is not a large sample; the portrayals of these
shields and their users in battle are greatly outnumbered by the
pictures of them being carried in neutral contexts, by files of men
on foot (Figure 40, lower zone) or in chariot processions. Yet the
record remains a curiously one-sided one, with thirteen definite

and three probable defeats out of sixteen. It seems to me likely that the painters of the dozen battle scenes from which these figures are taken were trying to characterize the users of these shields in some way, at least when it came to combat, and that their meaning was intelligible at least in the small circle of their known customers. The likelihood of mere coincidence is further reduced by another feature pointed out by Coldstream in his review: in no single surviving Geometric battle scene is the same type of shield carried by members of *opposing* sides. What I am suggesting is not that the context of these scenes need necessarily therefore be heroic; but that they are likely to have a narrative content of some kind.

Let us turn back now to the question of the treatment of time, which we saw to be bound up with the understanding of later Greek vase-paintings and works of art of other kinds. I have tried to show elsewhere that Geometric scenes, of varying subject matter, exhibit rudimentary instances of the "synoptic" method, in which we can say that more than one moment of time (or on the other account, more than one "epithet") appears in the same picture.[20] Even the commonest of subjects, the *prothesis*, shows this in a number of cases. Twice, the actual lying in state appears in the same zone as a complete procession of chariots; more often, a few representative chariots (as in Figures 39 and 42) appear immediately alongside the *prothesis*, rather than the full procession.[21] In any sensible funerary ritual, these two events would take place successively, not simultaneously, so that the participants could witness both; furthermore they must have been spatially separated, with the procession in a large open space and the lying in state either indoors or in the courtyard of the deceased's house.

20. A. M. Snodgrass, *Narration and Allusion in Archaic Greek Art* (cited above, n. 5), 16–21.

21. See *Prothesis and Ekphora* (cited above, n. 16), 185, on nos. 20 and 33, noting also 160–70 on "the lateral extensions of the prothesis zone."

Figure 42. Fragment of Attic Geometric krater (Athens), with scene of *prothesis*.

Parallel arguments could be applied to the case of an actual procession where the chariot passengers face alternately forwards and backwards,[22] which is best explained as showing different moments in the course of a ritual that required them to turn around as the chariot raced along; to pictures of dancers, some of whom have their hands raised and some lowered, which are susceptible of a parallel explanation; and to a few of the small, but interesting, group of Geometric scenes that have been thought to show specific legends, known to us from epic or other literary sources—including both the examples to be discussed presently (Figures 45 and 48). Nor is this "proto-synoptic" idea the only link between Geometric and later artists' approaches to their themes. A group of later paintings with genre subjects treats the theme of the dance in a quite different way, by choosing the fleeting moment of time in which a dancer is in the act of leaping into the air, with legs doubled underneath him (Figure 43). It is remarkable to find that there is more than one example of this motif in Geometric vase-painting, showing a preoccupation with

22. Amphora, Hamburg 1966.89: see *Prothesis and Ekphora* (cited above, n. 16), 28, 189–90, no. 43, pl. 60a.

Figure 43. Corinthian aryballos (Corinth Museum), with scene of dancers.

catching the single instant of time, almost in the manner of a snapshot (Figure 44).[23]

There is little doubt that further search would add considerably to this list of features that link the Geometric figure-scenes with those of the later phases of Greek art. But let us pause here to consider what has emerged so far. The Geometric vase-painter, almost from the time that he begins to show grouped figures, exhibits signs of what was later to become a consuming interest, that of embodying some kind of story in his compositions—whatever the precise content of those stories. He also makes use—indeed, it is only because of this that we can detect a narrative element in some of his pictures—of a technique that enables him to encapsulate more than one element of a narrative sequence in the same picture: the technique that I have been call-

23. For example, the kantharoi Athens NM 14447 and Copenhagen 727: see R. Tölle, *Frühgriechische Reigentänze* (Waldsassen, 1964), 12–14, nos. 4 (pl. 3) and 6.

Figure 44. Attic Geometric kantharos (Copenhagen), with scene of musicians and dancers.

ing "synoptic." Thus, whether or not we may infer from the use of this technique a *conscious* concern with the time-dimension, this conclusion seems to follow: whatever motive lay behind the use of the technique in Archaic and later times, that motive was already operative in the later part of the eighth century B.C., when the Geometric figure-scenes appeared.

I make these observations mainly in order to combat the tendency, long maintained among historians of classical art, to draw a firm line between Geometric and later art. This demarcation underlies many treatments of artistic questions, including the one from which we began, that of the narrative emphasis in Greek art. Specialists in this field have espoused the view that the Geometric painter, lacking the technical means of making explicit his narrative intentions, must therefore have lacked such intentions in the first place. It must be conceded that for us today (and therefore, we are apt to infer, for contemporaries too), it is only with great difficulty that any distinctive story can be extracted from these impersonal compositions. But I am not sure that this has any firm implications for the painters' thought-processes. I do not think that we should easily reject the view, put forward in Richard Kannicht's recent paper, that "for the contemporary (as well as for the modern) viewer they were (as they are) open to more than one interpretation."[24] It is interesting that recent work of a Structuralist bent has begun to make some rather similar claims for vase-scenes of a later date,[25] and there is an attraction about any initiative that opens up the possibility of analogy between different periods of Greek art.

A good and specific example of this distinction habitually drawn between Geometric and later art—even art of the *immediately* ensuing generation—is given by the case of the strange "double figures" shown on a surprising number of Geometric vases (Figure 45). It is a widely held view, first advanced by John Cook in 1935 and strongly maintained by more recent writers, that the double figure is an artistic convention for showing two men (most often, two warriors) standing side by side.[26] This view fits well with the fact that, among other things, it appears four times on a single vessel, a krater in New York. But most adherents of this view have also seen that in the immediate post-Geometric period, the first decades of the seventh century B.C., the same convention (or something very like it) had already come

24. R. Kannicht, "Poetry and Art: Homer and the Monuments Afresh," *Classical Antiquity* 1 (1982): 85, a view anticipated by H.-P. Isler, "Zur Hermeneutik früher griechischer Bilder," in *Zur griechische Kunst: Hansjoerg Bloesch zum 60. Geburtstag* (*Ant. K.*, suppl. 9, Bern, 1973), 34–41.

25. As for instance those by C. Bérard, "Iconographie—Iconologie—Iconologique," *Etudes de Lettres* (1983), pt. 4, 5–37, for fountain-house scenes on hydriai (22) and for tyrannicide pictures on funerary vases (30–31); echoed by V. Dasen's paper (cited above, n. 9) in the same issue, at 68; note, too, R. Osborne, "The Myth of Propaganda and the Propaganda of Myth," *Hephaistos* 5–6 (1983–84):61–70.

26. J.M. Cook, "Protoattic pottery," *BSA* 35 (1934–35):206: "nothing more than the creation of artists faced with the difficulty of filling a space too broad for a single figure and too narrow for two." Cf. Boardman, "Symbol and Story" (cited above, n. 15), 25–26.

Figure 45. Projected drawing, by Piet de Jong, of scene from Attic Geometric oenochoë (Athens, Agora Museum).

to mean something quite different: it was now used to portray the pair of Siamese twins who occur in Greek legend, the sons of Aktor, who beat Nestor in a chariot race on one occasion, fought inconclusively against him on another, and were finally killed by Herakles. Now whatever our verdict on this theory, it clearly posits a certain perceptual gap or discontinuity between the Geometric artists and their immediate successors: a gap that would be quite intelligible—and would indeed find many parallels—if the two groups had belonged to different cultures, or even possessed different bodies of legend. But neither circumstance applies to this period of early Greek history.

I have been stressing, in contrast, certain elements of continuity between Geometric and later vase-painters. It would be unwarranted to use this evidence as a basis for the wider claim that there was also continuity in *subject matter* between the two periods: that, for example, the later preoccupation with portraying specific legends was already present in Geometric times. It is surely a sounder approach to examine the Geometric evidence first in its own framework, remembering that it reflected the concerns of a particular society—in some cases, as we have seen, a decidedly restricted society, but more generally the Greek communities of the later eighth century, about which we know a certain amount from other sources. One such source (a fundamental one) is our knowledge of the contemporary Greek language itself. I wish to digress here, to consider an important question that must arise in any discussion of attitudes to the heroic past: namely the meanings of the word *hērōs* itself.

In his edition of Hesiod's *Works and Days* in 1978, Martin West spelled out some of the implications of the curious fact, noted by Erwin Rohde more than eighty years earlier, that the word *hērōs* appears in Greek in two distinct, and in some ways incompatible, meanings.[27] In epic, it is freely applied to living men who are, before all else, warriors, but who when they eventually die or are killed, will pass irrevocably into a dim underworld. This use, which occurs seventy-four times in the *Iliad* alone, is also found in surviving passages of Hesiod as well as in the *Odyssey*—where, however, it is more indiscriminately applied (to a bard and a servant, for instance), in a way that might suggest that this sense for *hērōs* had now begun to pass out of the living language. By contrast, *hērōs* in later literature means someone who has died—not necessarily long ago, but sometimes very recently—but who in another sense has been immortalized, and is honored by some kind of cult. The first sense is thus purely secular, the second essentially religious. The two senses are not, however, sequential in time, as the literary record might suggest: if anything, there are signs that the second use of *hero*, though not attested in writing until the later accounts of the Code of Draco (c. 620 B.C.), may be the older and the more primitive. Rather, they represent two different facets of a system, developed separately during the Greek Early Iron Age; West tentatively hints at a *geographical* distinction between the two in the earlier stages, with the secular warrior-hero being characteristic of the Ionian epic, and the hero of cult being at home in the Greek mainland. The archaeological evidence certainly supports the second element of this view, with the practice of cult-offerings at the

27. See M. L. West, *Hesiod: The Works and Days* (Oxford, 1978), 186 on line 141; 190–91 on lines 159–60; and in excursus 1, 370–73. E. Rohde's discussion is to be found in his *Psyche: Seelencult und Unsterblichkeitsglaube der Griechen* (2nd ed., Freiburg i.B., Leipzig, and Tübingen, 1898), 152–99.

graves of the ancient or recent dead beginning very early on the mainland. In 1979 this same distinction in the use of the word *hero* was dealt with independently, and more elaborately, in an important book by Gregory Nagy.[28] He emphasized a further aspect of the contrast: the hero of Ionian epic is typically a figure of pan-Hellenic importance, whereas the status of the recipient of a hero-cult, like the cult itself, is usually a local one. The first is indeed "immortalized" in one sense, by having his deeds perpetuated in song, but the second becomes "immortal" in a more practical way, receiving honors almost as if he were a god. Nagy, like West, sees the two systems as having eventually come into some degree of competition; the result was a form of multiple fusion, with Homeric heroes, for example, also becoming recipients of a hero-cult.

Is this matter relevant to the interpretation of the Geometric vase-paintings of the Greek mainland? There has been a strong tradition here of pursuing parallels between the painter and the epic poet, not just at the level of their general mentalities, but in terms of their interest in identical narrative subjects. I count this, however, among those approaches referred to earlier, which must be judged to have failed. I was glad to read in John Boardman's recent paper the bald proposition "that no Attic Geometric artist had ever read or heard recited a single line of Homer."[29] On a parallel issue, that of the Geometric hero-cults at anonymous Bronze Age graves, I have argued likewise that the absolute contradiction between the funerary practices described by Homer and those of the actual mainland tombs where cults were established hardly suggests that the latter activity was inspired by hearing epic recitations.[30] On reflection, I now feel that this

28. G. Nagy, *The Best of the Achaeans* (Baltimore, 1979), pt. 2, 69–210, especially 114–17, 159–61.

29. Boardman, "Symbol and Story" (cited above, n. 15), 29.

30. See A. M. Snodgrass, "Les Origines du culte des héros dans la Grèce antique," in *La Mort, les morts dans les sociétés anciennes*, ed. G. Gnoli and J.-P. Vernant (Cambridge, 1982), 107–19, especially 115–16. There has per-

view could have been put more strongly: the contrast between the cremation, covered by a tumulus, that Homer describes and the multiple inhumations in rock-cut chamber-tombs where most of the cults were instituted is so complete that it positively *excludes* familiarity with Homer—or, at least, identification of the object of the cult with a "Homeric hero."

Now, too, it becomes possible to fit a new piece of evidence into its place. Greek hero-cult, as already remarked, could include not only the worship of the remote and anonymous Bronze Age dead but also the heroization of the recently deceased. The discovery in 1981 of a pair of exceptionally rich burials of the tenth century B.C. at Lefkandi, over which a large building (Figure 54, p. 183), apparently a *hērōön* (center of hero-cult), had been almost at once constructed,[31] posed insuperable problems for those who believed in the influence of Ionian epic on such practices: for who could believe that the great burial scenes in Homer, or even their earlier prototypes, were known to the people of the island of Euboea as early as about 950 B.C.? We can now see this phenomenon for what it probably is: an unusually early manifestation of a strand of hero worship that we know well from classical times—the elevation of prominent persons to the ranks of the heroes immediately after their death. Rohde, who called the hero-cults of classical Greece "a still burning spark of ancient belief kindled to a new flame," spoke truer than he knew: the spark had been alight since at least the tenth century B.C. (*Psyche*, W. B. Hillis, trans.).

---

haps been an excess of recent writing on this theme, as is shown by the fact that some of the same points are made in an earlier paper of mine, "Poet and Painter in Eighth-century Greece," *PCPS* 205 (1979):118–30; by Kannicht, "Poetry and Art," in 1982 (cited above, n. 25); and again by C. Brillante, "Episodi iliadici nell'arte figurata e conoscenza dell'*Iliade* nella Grecia antica," *Rh. Mus.* 126 (1983): 97–125—three articles none of which displays awareness of the others.

31. See M. R. Popham, E. Touloupa, and L. H. Sackett, "The Hero of Lefkandi," *Antiquity* 56 (1982): 169–74.

Figure 46. Distribution map of hero-cults in early Greece.

We can now begin to draw the strands of this argument together. The worship of the anonymous but heroic dead (Figure
46), that essentially local phenomenon, was part of the world
view of several eighth-century communities in mainland Greece:
notably in the Peloponnese (the Corinthia, the Argolid [Figure
47], and later Messenia); but also perhaps in Boeotia (on the evidence of a passage of Hesiod to be considered in a moment); and
quite definitely in Attica (the most relevant locality from the
point of view of the Geometric vase-paintings). The evidence
here includes one of the richest of these cults, at the Mycenaean
tholos-tomb of Menidhi (ancient Acharnai), where as Peter Kahane shrewdly pointed out, the dedications actually included
Geometric vases decorated with racing chariots in a funerary

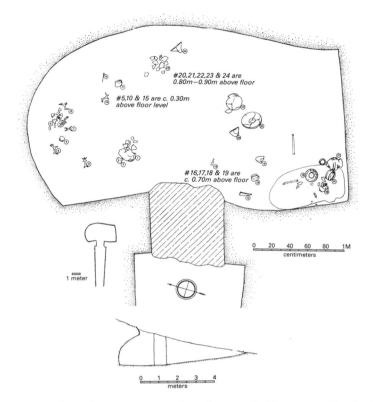

Figure 47. Plan of a Mycenaean chamber-tomb (Prosymna Tomb xix) with traces of later cult (after C. W. Blegen).

context.[32] The very foundation of the Olympic Games, traditionally in 776 B.C., may be linked with such practices. Euboea, as we have seen, provides our earliest evidence for the heroization of the newly deceased, and the occurrence at Lefkandi is supported by a later instance from nearby Eretria.[33] Quite possibly,

32. P. P. Kahane, "Ikonologische Untersuchungen zur griechisch-geometrischen Kunst," *Ant. K.* 16 (1973): 134 n. 89.

33. See C. Bérard, "Récupérer la mort du prince," in *La Mort, les morts* (cited above, n. 30), 89–105.

the subjects of these early cults were, at the time, referred to by some word other than *hero*: just as, in the converse case, Homer seems to prefer the word *hēmitheos* ("demigod") for those few personages in his poems who appear to receive worship after their deaths. It seems to have been in the years round 700 B.C., with the fusion of the two facets of heroism, that the local grave-cults were joined by the worship of the named heroes of epic, ranging from the famous Agamemnon and Menelaos to the more obscure Phrontis, who had been Menelaos's steersman and was probably commemorated at Cape Sunion, where he had died. It may be significant, too, that these "Homeric" cults seem never to be located at genuine graves of the heroic age.

We return now to a point made much earlier, about the social and chronological exclusiveness of the vases with battle scenes from Athenian burials. It has emerged that the background of the people who made and used these vases is unlikely to have been touched by Ionian epic. It may indeed be doubted whether their vision was shaped by literary works of any kind, but that is not central to the argument here. Whether we are dealing with lost poetry, or with a purely vernacular oral tradition, the content of the stories familiar to these people is likely, from our point of view and indeed from that of post-Homeric Greece, to have been of considerable obscurity. The legends will have included a sub-stantial body of primarily local traditions, of the kind that often surfaces in later classical literature, sometimes to the embarrass-ment of the writers who retail it, because of its predictable incon-sistency with the (by then) more widely accepted versions. It is no wonder, then, that the attempt to match the pictures on their vases with the episodes known from epic has been a failure: no wonder, but also no reflection on the likelihood of legendary sub-jects having been portrayed.

We have, in the course of this argument, reached two appar-ently conflicting conclusions: on the one hand the Geometric art-ists, in terms of their techniques and aims, show signs of having begun to explore the same problems that preoccupied their successors; but on the other, they cannot be thought to have yet encountered the inspiration from epic that was to make a progressively greater impact on those successors in their choice of subject matter. The question of the subjects of the Geometric vase-scenes is thus left in a state of suspense from which it may never be possible to release it. A possible view would be to see these paintings as a fleeting apparition in the history of ancient art; as the product of a brief overlap in time between the mainland Greek vision, not yet overlaid by the influence of epic, and the existence of a new conceptual apparatus that enabled a story to be told in visual form. If so, one could reasonably speculate that current beliefs included such elements as we know to have composed the traditional cult of the hero: the retailing of locally important legend and its linkage with the honors paid to the remote and anonymous dead. This is the spirit embodied by the passage in Hesiod's *Works and Days* (lines 141–43), in which he speaks of the tribute paid after their death, *not* to the heroes, but to the Silver Men of a yet earlier age: hidden under the earth, they have become "spirits of the underworld," and they are remembered with honor. But the tradition also extended to the more recent dead, and some fusion may have taken place between these and their more distant predecessors, in that "highly evolved transformation of the worship of ancestors" that Nagy (following Rohde) sees in the Greek cult of heroes.[34]

If any of this belief infiltrated the decoration of the Geometric vases, it would of course make for a much more ambiguous interpretation of them than those sought by modern scholarship. It is unlikely that we shall ever be able to assess the relative prominence, in the mind of artist and client, of the several elements in this "evolved ancestor worship." Moreover, we cannot exclude the possibility that such an interpretation might apply, not only to the relatively frequent and apparently anonymous crowd

34. Nagy, *Best of the Achaeans* (cited above, n. 28), 115.

Figure 48. Attic Geometric bowl (London, British Museum), with scene of departing warship.

scenes on which we have been concentrating, but also to the handful of more distinctive pictures in which elements of a *unique* narrative content have been seen. Because of the obvious attraction of identifying their subjects with episodes known from epic, these few pictures have become the fiercest battleground between the upholders of the "heroic" interpretation and their more skeptical opponents.

A notable case in point has been the scene on a bowl in London showing a departing warship; it perhaps belongs to the 730s B.C. (Figure 48). Klaus Fittschen, for example, devoted several pages to arguing that it could not be interpreted as a portrayal of the elopement of Helen with Paris, of the abduction of Ariadne by Theseus, or of the flight of Jason with Medea, all of which identifications had been earlier suggested.[35] But what if we look

35. K. Fittschen, *Untersuchungen zum Beginn der Sagendarstellungen bei den Griechen* (Berlin, 1969), 51–60.

Figure 49. Impression of a gold signet ring (Oxford, Ashmolean Museum), said to be from the harbor town of Knossos.

at it in the different, if hazier, light of a society known to have been concerned with hero and ancestor worship? We might then wish to compare its iconography with that of a surviving Bronze Age scene to which it bears a certain resemblance: the one on a Minoan gold ring from the harbor town of Knossos (Figure 49).[36] The subject of the gold ring is detectably different: the man and woman at the left do not seem to be about to embark on the galley in this case, whereas the man at least is definitely going to do so in the Geometric scene; and a female figure, doubtless a goddess, appears to float in the air above the Minoan ship. But some iconographic connection, however indirect, would go some way towards explaining a puzzling feature of the Geometric painting, the large scale of the figures at the left; and the very existence of such a connection would be suggestive for the interpretation of the later work.

At this point, the skeptics may appeal to the verdict of the late V. E. G. Kenna (see n. 38 below) that the ring is, or may be, a modern forgery. His opinion was based partly on the suspiciously excellent preservation of the work, partly on the icono-

36. Oxford, Ashmolean Museum no. 1938.1129.

Figure 50. Impression of a gold signet ring (Athens, National Museum), from the Tiryns Treasure.

graphic resemblance to other ancient works (perhaps including our Geometric bowl) that could have been known to a forger in 1927, the year in which Sir Arthur Evans first came to hear of the ring's existence. But the scene on the ring does have some affinity, in content but not in style (as, less directly, does the Geometric vase-painting) with another gold ring of Bronze Age date, which cannot be suspected of being a forgery, since it was dug up as part of a hoard at Tiryns in 1915 (Figure 50).[37] Furthermore, the genuineness of the Knossos harbor town ring had been accepted by a long line of experts before Kenna, including not merely Evans (who had the vested interest of having later bought it), but also Martin Nilsson in 1928, Axel Persson in 1942, Hagen Biesantz in 1954 (by implication, since he excluded it from his list of *gemmae dubitandae*), and Stylianos Alexiou, who proposed a new interpretation of it in 1958. Fittschen, writing in 1969, did not use this pretext for disregarding the ring, as well as the one from Tiryns, but merely remarked (quite correctly) that since their own interpretation was obscure, they could not be used to aid

37. See G. Karo, "Schatz von Tiryns," *AM* 55 (1930): 124–26, pls. 2.2 and 3.1 and Beilage 30.1: no. 6209.

the interpretation of the Geometric scene.[38] My point can be summed up by saying that a connection of any kind between the Geometric painting and the Minoan ring—provided that the latter is genuine—will be enough to throw grave doubt on what has become the standard skeptical reading of the Geometric scene: that it portrays a blameless eighth-century Athenian sea-captain saying good-bye to his wife.

But there I should like to leave the matter. The general aim of this chapter has not been to interpret: indeed, it could be seen as that of showing that interpretation is premature, and that our failure to achieve any consensus to date is itself a sign of this prematureness. We have first to establish something more fundamental: the general *area* in which we might conduct our search in the future for possible interpretations of the baffling figure-scenes of Greek Geometric art.

38. On the Knossos harbor town ring, see Persson, *Religion of Greece* (cited above, n. 7), 81–82, ring no. 26; and also S. Alexiou, "O daktulios tēs Oxfordis," in *Minoica: Festschrift zum 80. Geburtstag von Johannes Sundwall*, ed. E. Grumach (Berlin, 1958), 1–5, who cites the earlier verdicts on the ring's genuineness and detects a parallel resemblance to another work of post-Minoan date, the open-work bronze stand from the Idaean Cave. For later views, see V. E. G. Kenna, *Cretan Seals* (Oxford, 1960), 154, under both "3(b)" and "7(a)"; Fittschen, *Untersuchungen* (cited above, n. 35), 58 and n. 307. I am most indebted to J. G. Younger, who is to include the ring in a forthcoming publication and has drawn my attention to features (the form of the ring itself, the decoration on the ship's hull) that would not have been likely to occur to a forger in or before 1927.

CHAPTER SIX

The Early Iron Age of Greece

This chapter sets out to present a study in synthesis, as tentative and provisional as the attempt at analysis offered in the preceding chapter. One of the objectives of archaeology according to David Clarke—indeed perhaps its highest objective—is "the development of higher category knowledge or principles that synthesize and correlate the material in hand while possessing a high predictive value."[1] In proposing a few hesitant steps towards that rather lofty aim, I choose for a field the Early Iron Age. I personally have done intermittent work on this period for some time, but I hope to show that it also has more objective qualifications to serve as the field for such an experiment.

As its name suggests, the period between about 1100 and 700 B.C. witnessed the introduction of a new industrial metal to take the place of bronze. But it is also distinguished from the Late Bronze Age by a whole series of other criteria. First, the greater part of it appears to have been an entirely illiterate age, whereas the Late Bronze Age had seen the development of at least two comprehensive writing systems in one or more centers of Aegean culture. Further, the secondary capacity for communication pro-

1. D. L. Clarke, *Analytical Archaeology* (London, 1968; 2nd ed. 1978, ed. R. Chapman), 20.

170

vided by representational art was also temporarily lost at the transition from Late Bronze to Early Iron. Next, the marginally historical quality that the Late Bronze Age acquires from the fact that there are probable references to the Aegean world in surviving Hittite and Egyptian documents is also missing from the ensuing age. Fourth, the core of Late Bronze Age historical reality that has been argued—one might say demonstrated—to lie behind later Greek heroic legend has no counterpart in the Early Iron Age: insofar as any legends can be argued to have their origins in these centuries, they are (like the foundation traditions of the Ionian migration) utterly impoverished in content compared with the great sagas that have maintained their grip on the ensuing three millennia. Turning to strictly archaeological evidence, the record of military disturbance, and provision against it, that makes the Late Bronze Age such a convincing setting for the heroic legends is not continued into the Early Iron Age: destructions of settlements are hardly attested until the eighth century, and even fortifications seem entirely confined to Ionia and the islands of the Aegean. Indeed, the use of monumental masonry, for any purpose, disappears for some centuries after the end of the Bronze Age. Finally, we may in effect sum up several of the preceding observations by saying that the later Greeks seem neither to have remembered, nor to have wished to invent, many events or personalities that could be attributed to the Early Iron Age. The very few exceptions are, among the personalities, suspect either as to their very existence, or at least in terms of their chronological placing in some Greek sources: I am thinking of such cases as Herodotus's ninth-century date for Hesiod and Homer, or the galaxy of early dates offered for Lykourgos of Sparta. As for the "events," most of them are (like the Ionian migration) really only prolongations of the long-drawn-out processes of migration that had characterized the end of the Bronze Age.

Yet the Early Iron Age, while so clearly set off from what had preceded it, cannot be regarded simply as the beginning of the new era of historical Greek civilization either: it is too sharply divided from the Archaic period that followed it. One category of this division was considered in chapter 5: the transformation in the whole attitude to the heroic past that came about with the westward spread of Ionian epic. Prior to this, it seems that on the Greek mainland (and at least some offshore islands) the idea of the "hero" was linked to ancestor worship, and was not tied to one specific past era; afterwards, these attitudes had to be merged with the notion of an eternally receding "Heroic Age," set already in the distant past, and a prime heritage of the whole Greek world.

Beside this division of an intellectual and spiritual kind, we can set several others that are on a more mundane level. There is, first, a remarkable discontinuity in occupation between what appear to be some of the most prominent settlement sites of the Early Iron Age and those of the ensuing period. There is an obvious commonsense objection here: that it is the very fact that these sites *were* deserted after the Early Iron Age that has made them fruitful sources of knowledge for the excavators interested in this early period. There is some force in this claim: undoubtedly there are also sites famous from later ages, such as Athens and Argos, that would be prime sources of information about the Early Iron Age were it not for the disturbance and contamination of their earlier levels brought about by their later florescence. But there remains a core of reality that cannot be entirely eroded by this argument. There is a long list of important Early Iron Age settlement and cemetery sites that simply disappeared from recorded history after this period ended: the telltale sign here is that they are known to us, and will always have to be known, by their modern Greek place-names. But it would be difficult to claim that all, or even most, of the places on this list are important only in the sense that they convey important knowledge to the archaeologist. Among them are Karphi, Kavousi, Vrokastro, and Kommos in Crete; in the Cyclades, Zagora on Andros, Xobourgo on Tenos, Agios Andreas on Siphnos, Koukounaries on Paros, Grotta on Naxos, and the site called Vathy Limenari on tiny Donoussa; further east, Emborio on Chios and Vroulia on Rhodes (even though both survived into the earlier Archaic period); Lefkandi in Euboea; and on the mainland, Nichoria in Messenia and Kalapodi in Phokis (see Figures 56–58, pp. 186 and 191). Some of these had at least a genuine regional importance: Zagora for example was surely for a time the leading settlement on Andros; Koukounaries has in the past two years of excavation shown itself to have been a much larger site than had previously been apparent; Kommos has remarkable architectural features for its period; Kalapodi was clearly an important sanctuary for its region; and as for Lefkandi, on present showing it had features unmatched in the whole of the then Greek world.

Yet these places were eventually abandoned, in most cases totally and permanently, and then forgotten. Whatever our explanation of this fact, it is likely to include an acknowledgment that the nature and needs of a major regional settlement site were no longer commensurate with some of the sites of the preceding era. This circumstance thus provides a major distinction between the Early Iron Age and succeeding periods. It is not the only such feature. At approximately the same date as that of the abandonment of many of these places—that is, about the end of the eighth century—other changes are visible in the sites where occupation does continue, whether we choose to treat them as the culmination of the Early Iron Age or as signs of the advent of something new. Some are merely the positive counterparts of the features listed earlier, in their negative form, for the end of the Bronze Age: the recovery of writing, for example, the return of representational art in a variety of media, and the resurgence of some kind of continuous historical, or pseudo-historical, record. In the archaeological field, we now have independent evidence that organized internal warfare was once again becoming the normative state of affairs in mainland Greece; this was also the time when burial with arms, that symbol of private, free-lance militarism, was discontinued in the more advanced regions of Greece.

These two balancing sets of contrasts would appear, from the viewpoint of the traditional historian or archaeologist, to show the Early Iron Age at a disadvantage at every turn. The reconstruction of a narrative history, which is a temptation for the archaeologist of the Aegean Bronze Age and a duty for the traditional classicist, is simply an impossibility for the Early Iron Age archaeologist. Even for an analysis of the society of the period, in default of the kind of secondary aid that can elsewhere be acquired from Linear B texts or Archaic inscriptions and vase-paintings, one must depend on various archaeological approaches that are, as yet, in an early stage of their development; for recent analyses have suggested that the Homeric poems, that other potential resource, are as debatable in their application to these questions as are, say, the Geometric vase-paintings. Yet, negative though they mostly are, my reason for drawing up this list of characteristic features of the Early Iron Age is in fact an optimistic one.

I want to suggest that these very features give us the freedom to apply certain approaches most commonly adopted in much earlier periods of prehistory, and generally associated with the new archaeology. Such approaches proceed by first posing a clearly defined problem, rather than simply confronting a period or subject; by then developing a model that embraces specific assumptions that bear on that problem, rather than letting the evidence "speak for itself"; by then deducing certain testable propositions that should follow from the model, rather than merely looking for suggestive features in the evidence previously considered; and, finally, by actually testing those propositions. I do not promise to follow this procedure every step of the way; but I do think that we could make a beginning by choosing a problem that is so central to the Early Iron Age of Greece that our pro-

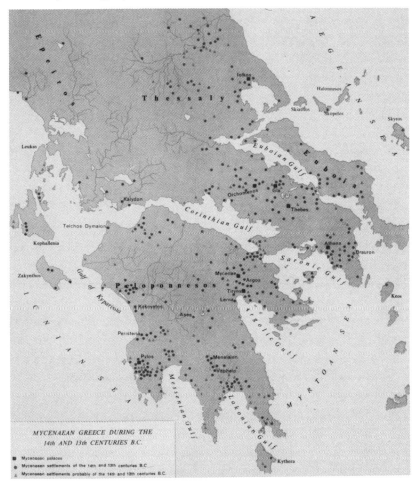

Figure 51. Distribution map of sites in Mycenaean Greece, fourteenth to thirteenth centuries B.C. (after G. Phylaktopoulos and C. Bastias).

posed solution to it will constitute a synthesis of some of the most important evidence available from that period.

This, of course, involves an act of choice. I have pondered and rejected a series of possible problems because, although real enough, they do not quite possess the quality of centrality that we are looking for. There is, for example, the well-worn question of what brought about the fall of the Late Bronze Age civilizations of the Aegean, reducing the populous and clearly stratified settlement pattern that we see in the map of Mycenaean Greece in the fourteenth and thirteenth centuries B.C. (Figure 51) to the fragmented remnant that appears in the map of sites known to be occupied in the later eleventh century, at the transition from the Bronze to the Iron Age (Figure 52). It is relevant that this *is* such a well-worn question, that so many variant solutions to it have been proposed that, collectively, they may already comprise a substantial element of the truth; relevant, but not decisive. A more important consideration is that, even if an entirely convincing account of this episode could be achieved, it would not constitute more than the first chapter in any synthesis of the nature of the Early Iron Age.

Next, and in some ways more attractive, there is the problem of the change in metal use itself: what were the causes and effects of the replacement of bronze by iron (Figure 53) as the staple material for a range—actually quite a narrow range, but a vital one—of industrial and other activities? Is it possible that the impact of this change was so deep that it shaped, to some considerable extent, the developments of the next few centuries? This approach would have the great advantage that, since virtually every part of Europe and Asia was in due course to go through much the same change, comparative evidence can be drawn from almost half the globe. This and other attractions have exercised a special appeal in Marxist circles, and Gordon Childe was probably the first to give an affirmative answer to the question that I asked just now: yes, the impact of the change affected every society that underwent it, to its foundations; the cheapness and wide availability of iron, by comparison with copper and tin, would have had an egalitarian and democratizing effect. Since just such an effect is, in some non-Marxist opinions, detectable in the material record of Early Iron Age Greece, the argument is by no means to be dismissed as mere dogma. The issue as a whole, too, must surely lie near to the heart of the matter. Yet as

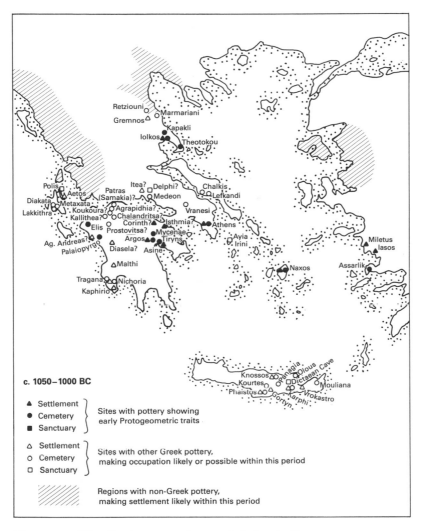

Figure 52. Distribution map of occupied sites in Greece, c. 1050–1000
B.C.

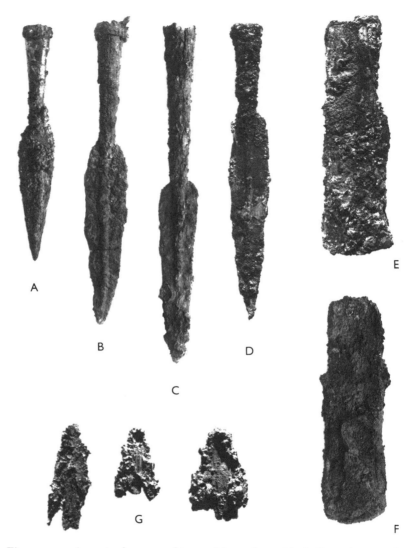

Figure 53. A typical range of iron objects from Early Iron Age tombs (Lefkandi, Euboea).

an explanatory model for the Early Iron Age, it has one defect that appears insurmountable: as it stands, it may explain some of the striking contrasts with the Late Bronze Age, but *not* those with the ensuing Archaic and classical periods, in which Greek industry and economy remained essentially based on iron, yet took radically different forms.

I turn therefore to a third possible approach: that which is based on the political systems of the Early Iron Age. Is it possible to reconstruct them, through a combination of inferences from the breakdown of the Late Bronze Age systems (of which we know a little), from the contemporary archaeological evidence, and from possible survivals of the Early Iron Age systems into later periods? To a limited extent, I think that it may be; but I do not think that this approach can generate enough *explanatory* power. Even if we succeeded in establishing, say, that Greece in the Early Iron Age was peopled by a network of acephalous tribal societies with few distinctions of rank and wealth—and I doubt that we can—then this would still remain for the most part a result, not a cause, of more fundamental processes that would remain obscure.

I therefore suggest that we formulate our problem in none of the aforementioned ways. The weakness of the approach through the fall of the Bronze Age civilizations is that it can throw light only on the beginning of the Early Iron Age, and not on its duration. The approach through the change in metals might explain why some features of the period took the form that they did, but not why there was such a long delay before they developed into something quite different. The approach through political systems could hardly have a temporal dimension at all, given the paucity and imprecision of direct evidence. In other words, all three approaches fail in respect of the *length* of the period that possessed the features we are trying to explain. Might we therefore instead directly address the issue of duration? The problem could then be posed as follows: why did it come about that some four centuries elapsed during which Greek material culture appears to have changed so little? Why did it take so long for literacy, representational art, monumental architecture, and other attributes to appear, or reappear, in the form in which they eventually did? Why were the later Greeks apparently content to accept so long an interruption in their recorded past?

I have tried to avoid phrasing these questions in a prejudicial way, by stressing the *appearance* rather than the actuality of the material record. Another of the lessons that we should be learning from the new archaeology is the urgent need for developing what Lewis Binford calls "Middle Range Theory": a theory, that is, for relating the apparent features of the archaeological record to the realities that caused them to appear in that form. He writes: "We need . . . to get answers to questions such as 'What does it mean?' and 'What was it like?' Only if reliable answers to these questions can be obtained might work on the question 'Why did it happen?' be profitable."[2] Since this last is indeed the form of question that we are posing ourselves, it will be as well to pay heed. We cannot naively assume that the material record of our period means what it appears to mean; nor can we evade the problems by simply posing *all* our questions in terms of the appearance of the evidence today, for the answers, whether they proved trivial or interesting, would not advance the main argument. Somehow, we have to take the intervening step from the record as it appears in the 1980s to the material realities of the time.

As often, we who work in Greece are relatively lucky, by the standards of world archaeology, in the range of external, nonarchaeological evidence to which we can appeal. In the present

2. L. R. Binford, *In Pursuit of the Past* (London, 1983), 194. Also important is his argument (e.g., at 213) that the use of evidence from nonarchaeological contexts is vitally necessary to the development of archaeological "Middle Range Theory," rather than being merely a passing fashion among new archaeologists as some of their critics believe.

quandary, too, we can make use of this circumstance. Thanks to the Linear B texts, we know that speakers of the Greek language were living at least in the central and southern Greek mainland and Crete in the Late Bronze Age. We know that in these and many other regions they also comprised at least the overwhelming majority of the population in the eighth and seventh centuries B.C. We are thus entitled to infer that, to a considerable degree, it was one and the same people that generated the material record from the earlier to the later period, passing through the Early Iron Age on the way. If it was essentially the same people who apparently lost the art of writing and then rediscovered it in a different form; gave up producing representational art in several media and then resumed doing so, partly in these same media; abandoned monumental building in dressed masonry and then adopted it again—if this is so, then it would seem reasonable to infer that there was some profound change of circumstances that led to the suspension of practices that, earlier and later, were found appropriate to life in Greek lands.

Let us suppose, however, that some or all of these "interruptions" are apparent and not real; that the changes in the record were brought about merely by changes in what David Clarke called "depositional behaviour."[3] In this case, there may have continued to be writing and representational art, but executed only in perishable materials; monumental masonry may have been used, but in entirely new contexts, where excavation has not yet detected it, or at least recognized it as belonging to this period. One might, perhaps, even then maintain that the inference of a "profound change in circumstances" could still stand: after all, could anything less induce people to alter their habits so radically? As a matter of fact, however, I think that we can go some way towards showing that our picture of the Early Iron Age is not so illusory.

3. D. L. Clarke, "Archaeology: The Loss of Innocence," *Antiquity* 47 (1973): 16.

With writing, for instance, it is not *just* the fact that for over four hundred years no trace of writing in durable materials survives. There is also the observation that the Linear B script, as seen in the late thirteenth century B.C., and the early alphabetic writing of the mid eighth century B.C. have absolutely no point of contact between them. Yet there was scope for such interaction: for Linear B, although a syllabic script, did have five signs for the five simple vowels *a, e, i, o* and *u* when used in an initial position. The devisers of the early Greek alphabets found that signs for these vowels were deficient in the Semitic models that they were otherwise using, and had therefore to designate signs for them. Had the Linear B script given way directly to these Greek alphabets, we might have expected there to be some vestigial relationship between the signs chosen, for essentially the same purpose, by the two writing systems; but there is no trace of any such thing. So although we must concede the possibility that the interval of illiteracy lasted considerably less than its apparent four hundred years, it is hard to believe that it will ever prove to have been nonexistent.

With monumental architecture one can argue along similar lines. We can be virtually certain, at any rate, that it did not continue in use for fortification, the context where it had previously been at perhaps its most impressive: not least because of the interesting cases where surviving Late Bronze Age fortifications were later brought back into use to protect Iron Age settlements. As for domestic buildings, we can point to at least one instance where the scale of the building would, in the eyes of a Mycenaean architect, have cried out for the use of a rectangular plan, timber reinforcement, and perhaps dressed masonry footings. It is the building identified by its excavators as a *hērōön* at Lefkandi, which was mentioned in the previous chapter (Figure 54).[4] It was well over 30 feet wide and at least 150 feet long—bigger than the

4. See M. R. Popham, E. Touloupa, and L. H. Sackett, "The Hero of Lefkandi," *Antiquity* 56 (1982): 169–74.

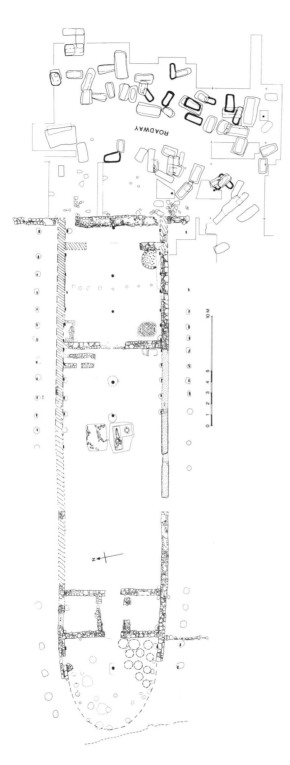

ROADWAY

0 1 2 3 4 5   10 M

Figure 54. Plan of the probable *hērōön* at Lefkandi, Euboea.

central building of a Mycenaean palace—yet its walls were constructed of a socle, or plinth, of roughly shaped stones with a mud-brick superstructure, and are only about two feet thick. It is not clear whether these features have anything to do with the extreme brevity of the building's life, estimated at a single generation.

If these are cases where there was a genuine interruption of traditional practice, we can add to them others where the argument from silence does not enter into the matter. It is a fact, for example, that at the close of the Bronze Age, large areas of the Greek mainland gave up multiple burial in collective tombs in favor of single burial, whether by interment (Figure 55) or with cremation; the record is continuous from one period into the next. Likewise, when we consider building plans rather than building materials, there is clear evidence from many sites that the apsidal plan (Figure 56) began to replace the rectangular one in the selfsame regions of the central and southern Greek mainland, sometimes directly overlying the rectilinear structures of the Late Bronze Age. In such instances, we surely have no need to devote time to the problem of whether these apparent changes really took place: we can instead address ourselves directly to the question of the *meaning* of the changes. Much the same could be said of the change in metal use that was referred to earlier: iron takes over directly from bronze for the same range of objects (primarily offensive weapons and edge-tools) found in the same kinds of context (primarily burials).

It is otherwise with the apparent depopulation of Greece in this period, also referred to earlier by implication (see p. 176 above). Here there are many potential factors that could have distorted the archaeological record: the fall in the number of occupied sites could be explained by greater nucleation, or by mass recourse to new sites in unexpected locations that have yet to be discovered; alternatively, there could be something seriously wrong with our chronological scheme, based on the sequence of

Figure 55. A typical cist grave of the Early Iron Age (Kerameikos SM grave 46, Athens).

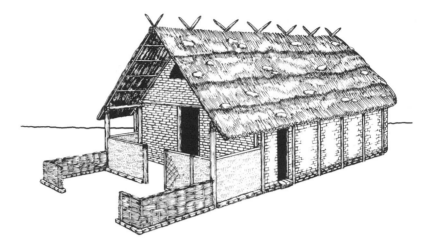

Figure 56. Reconstructed view of Early Iron Age apsidal house at Nichoria, Messenia (after W. A. McDonald and others).

styles of painted pottery. The fall in the number and frequency of burials could likewise be explained if some form of selectivity in burial was introduced at the close of the Bronze Age. These and other arguments have indeed been used by those who find the ostensible pattern, as presented for example in Figure 52, impossible to accept. It will be wiser, therefore, to confine ourselves to speaking of an *apparent* rather than a proven phenomenon here. But fortunately this may not in any case bear directly on our present enquiry: if, as most authorities now maintain, population level is an accompaniment, rather than a determinant, of major historical processes, then it follows that it cannot *explain* those processes, but can merely illustrate them.

We must return to the formulation of the chosen problem that faces us. What *was* the change of circumstance that caused Greek society, having lost literacy, abandoned many forms of representational art, and discontinued the use of monumental architecture and rectangular building plans, to endure these apparent deprivations for a period of centuries? What was it that, at the same period, led to the permanent substitution of iron for bronze, and the almost equally permanent change, in many areas, from collective tombs to single burial? What caused the apparent desertion, again for some centuries in most cases, of a large number of long-lived settlements? What, finally, prevented the inhabitants of Greece, during these same centuries, from achieving almost anything that was found worthy of commemoration by their descendants? Can we find Clarke's "principles that synthesize and correlate the material in hand while possessing a high predictive value"?

One starting assumption may perhaps be taken from recent work in nonclassical archaeology. Most modern explanations of change in cultures stress the *adaptive* element: innovation is seen, in many cases, as the result of a collective response, either to new needs or to changed conditions; whereas traditionally the same phenomena would have been attributed to conquest or immigration, or explained by assumptions about peculiar racial characteristics or even about the insights of outstanding individuals. It will be apparent that, for our problem in the form in which we have chosen to pose it, the new approach offers more than the traditional one: when it is the *persistence* of certain conditions that is in question, particularly if they are apparently unfavorable ones, greater explanatory power is obviously generated by a model of positive, adaptive accommodation to these conditions than by a single, once-for-all hypothesis about how the conditions came into being. To give two specific examples: it may be that the switch from rectangular to apsidal building plans reflects merely a loss of technical competence; or, perhaps better, the loss of a standard, centrally determined size of brick that had hitherto dictated building methods to some degree, and a consequent reversion to improvised practices, involving the substitution of *pisé* (rammed earth or mud) for individual bricks—as has recently been suggested.[5] Yet some further factor must be invoked to explain the prolonged delay in the resumption of former practices. Again, it *could* be that the advent of single burial reflects the arrival of new people for whom this was standard practice; but we must then still ask why the innovation commended itself to the Greeks, not only of the immediately ensuing generations in many parts of the country, but for much of the duration of classical civilization. Here, especially, the "adaptive" model is attractive: if the adoption of single burial is instead explained as a free choice on the part of people who no longer felt it appropriate for a family group to commit itself, by creating a collective tomb, to residence in one place for several generations, then one can see why the choice could have retained its appeal for later Greeks.

In the case of Early Iron Age Greece, I feel that past research (including my own—indeed perhaps especially my own) has placed too much stress on the negative aspects of the changes that took place near the beginning of this period. It now seems to me that the long duration of the responses and allegedly negative innovations demand that we look at the period in a different light. They must, in some important respects, have appeared to constitute a satisfactory solution to the conditions of life in Greece at the time. They must have composed a system that seemed to work reasonably well, even if that system had no features of interest to posterity, as was evidently the case.

What was that system like? Several kinds of evidence suggest that it was characterized by physical mobility. There are, first of all, the literary traditions of migration in at least the early phases of the period; but even those who embrace these traditions in all their detail as warmly as Nicholas Hammond does in the second edition of the *Cambridge Ancient History*,[6] for example, can only bring them to bear on the period down to about 1000 B.C.

5. G. Gullini, discussion intervention in *Annuario* 59 (1981): 344.
6. "The Literary Tradition of the Migrations," *CAH*, 2nd ed. (1975), vol. 2, pt. 2, 678–712.

There is also much archaeological evidence, again covering the twelfth and eleventh centuries B.C., to support the idea of a generally unsettled population: in the main, this indicates no more than local, short-range movements of people—but movements none the less. After this time, however, in the tenth, ninth, and eighth centuries, the orthodox view is that this unrest had come to an end, and that peaceful continuity of settlement, in the same locations, prevailed. But the time has perhaps come to question this view.

The prevalent picture of a settled country has, I think, arisen because movement of population is, in many minds, inseparable from war, invasion, and aggression generally. Since the evidence for these latter features—destruction levels, fortifications, and tangible innovations in material culture such as the advent of single burial—becomes very scarce in the years after about 1000 B.C., it has been tacitly inferred that population movements also came to an end. It must be conceded that there is a nucleus of major sites where the evidence does suggest more or less unbroken continuity from this time on: Athens, Argos, and Asine on the mainland and Knossos in Crete, for example; more questionably, Nichoria in Messenia and even more doubtfully Lefkandi in Euboea, where there are two mysterious gaps in the established sequence. When we look beyond these places, we find again and again that the evidence for occupation seems to begin or end, or both, with some abruptness at a point within the Early Iron Age.

Ideally, inferences of this kind should be based on excavated settlements; but the problem of necessarily incomplete excavation of sites, which was illustrated by the example of Lefkandi in chapter 2, makes this a hazardous undertaking. Still, we may point to a series of cases where the settlement is either relatively small and thoroughly excavated or, because of its later historical importance, has been fairly well scrutinized for signs of its earliest occupation. Of the places listed on pages 172–73 above, for

example, we find that the ninth century witnessed the first occupation of Zagora, Koukounaries, Vathy Limenari, and probably Xobourgo; by the same date or earlier, the first occupation
of the site of the city of Sparta seems to have taken place; later,
perhaps around 800, settlement began at another major classical
city, Eretria; the eighth century saw the occupation of Agios Andreas and Emborio (Figure 57) in the islands, and of a wide scatter of rural sites in Attica; now or earlier, the site of Messene was
occupied for the first time; latest of all, the site of Vroulia on
Rhodes (Figure 58) was settled around 700 B.C., just at the time
when the *abandonment* of some of the other island sites (Lefkandi, Zagora, Vathy Limenari) was beginning to happen.

We can reinforce this list of changes in settlement location by
referring to a number of cemetery sites with apparently limited
duration of use. Here, we must admit the possibility of other explanations of the interruptions besides the factor of incomplete
exploration: if, for example, it was a single lineage group that
made use of one grave plot, then the discontinuation of burial
may mean no more than the dissolution of that family group.
Even then, however, a shift of residence, if only at the individual
level, could well have resulted. At all events, it is a fact that many
of the most fully studied Early Iron Age cemeteries had a strictly
limited "life." In east-central Crete, the *tholos* cemetery at Pan-
agia and the cremations at Olous—both of them sites where the
burial evidence began only at the close of Minoan times—seem
to have gone out of use during the tenth century; a similar chronology applies to a series of cemeteries on the island of Kefallinía;
a burial tumulus at Vranesi (Agios Spyridon) in Boeotia was used
from the tenth to the early eighth centuries; in Thessaly, there are
substantial groups of graves at Halos, Marmariani, and Homo-
lion that likewise began in the tenth century, and were discontinued in the ninth or eighth.[7]

7. On these sites, see A. M. Snodgrass, *The Dark Age of Greece* (Edin-
burgh, 1971), chap. 4, with references there.

Figure 57. Reconstructed view of settlement at Emborio, Chios (after W. D. Heilmeyer).

Figure 58. Reconstructed view of settlement at Vroulia, Rhodes (after W. D. Heilmeyer).

This is an admittedly small sample of Iron Age sites—chosen, as I say, on the grounds of having been relatively thoroughly investigated—but it does tell a unified tale of relatively short-term occupation, preceded and/or terminated by an apparent movement of people, on however small a scale. If we except the sites of historical importance where settlement was to be permanent—Sparta, Eretria, Messene—the average "life" of this list of sites, settlements, and cemeteries, works out at some 150 years. This would be no fleeting period of time in contemporary eyes; yet it is significantly shorter than the average lifetime of a settlement in the preceding Bronze Age and, even more clearly, in the ensuing classical period. Whatever its ultimate significance, it is, I suggest, another of the distinctive features that help to set off the Early Iron Age as an interruption in the long-term development of Greek culture.

This finding may perhaps be brought into association with another, much more familiar aspect of Early Iron Age settlement: the relative rarity of sites of *any* kind. This is a feature that, far from being modified or diminished, has been greatly reinforced by the progress of Greek archaeology in the past decade. There are almost no new names, for example, to be added to the map shown in Figure 52, which was first published in 1971. The mainly negative results obtained by the time-honored method of excavation have been fully replicated by the more recent experience of surface survey, both extensive and intensive; some figures for Boeotia, to be considered presently, demonstrate this forcefully. As we have already acknowledged, this feature is not self-explanatory: other causes besides simple depopulation could lie behind the apparent lack of sites. In particular, now that we have the added finding that some of the sites that *were* occupied had limited lives, it begins to seem more likely that their mobility may also be partly responsible for the elusiveness of the inhabitants of Early Iron Age Greece; that this was at least a contributory cause. If people were readier to change their places of residence than at other periods, then their occupation of sites may have often been too fleeting for traces to be recoverable by excavation, let alone by surface survey.

What lay behind this disinclination to put down permanent roots, which apparently persisted for at least the two centuries between about 1100 and 900 B.C., when sites are so few, and in some areas even longer? Is it possible that the whole regime of sedentary occupation of more or less permanent sites that had characterized the Aegean world since Neolithic times—"sedentism," to give it a succinct, though hardly euphonious, label— was partially suspended during the Early Iron Age? Such a regime is, for obvious reasons, the normal accompaniment of an economy based on the plow; as has often been observed, it takes a lot to persuade peasants to desert their land. It may seem drastic to suggest that this tradition may have been interrupted, but in fact that view is very far from being original. It has regularly been asserted over the past fifty years of classical scholarship, though in most cases on purely a priori grounds, that Greek society in the period after the Mycenaean era reverted to some form of pastoralism.

Now a pastoralist community may take many forms. As a first step, we should acknowledge that the notion of *pure* pastoralism, for any period in later Mediterranean prehistory, and even on a local scale, is a highly improbable one. Most forms of animal husbandry are only effective within a context of wider farming: the availability of stubble for grazing in the later part of the year is only one of the reasons for this. As a strategy for subsistence, pastoralism is less reliable than cultivation, and of course it makes much greater territorial demands. Further, a pastoral community may be fundamentally as sedentary as one of cultivators; the difference is that, in the long term, pastoral use of the landscape tends gradually to exhaust it, and thus to encourage periodic changes of residence. The other alternatives are seasonal transhumance and a purely nomadic way of life; but I see no strong case for invoking either of these practices for the Greek Early Iron Age as a whole. Transhumant communities exist to this day in some of the lands round the Mediterranean, but only by positive and detailed arguments, of a kind requiring evidence that is simply not available for this period, could they be shown to have been a widespread phenomenon in past ages; while fully fledged nomadism is especially ill-suited to the fragmented landscape of the Aegean world, with its numerous mountain barriers, inlets, and islands. Let us then concentrate on the minimal hypothesis: that the Early Iron Age communities diverted a greater part of their resources to the pastoral sector than either their predecessors or their successors, and that this explains some of the distinctive features in the material record of this period.

We should deal at once with two objections of principle. First, this hypothesis posits a partial reversion from a more advanced to a more primitive method of exploiting the environment; and human communities who have once enjoyed the benefits of an agricultural economy do not lightly turn their backs on them. This line of reasoning has been strongly urged on me by those prehistorians to whom I have ventured to advance this idea in the past. For a time I was dismayed by this reaction: there could be no hope of convincing those who thought that the whole suggestion was to be excluded on principle. Yet what precisely is the principle that excludes it? In part, it rests on the disadvantageous features of pastoralism that have been sketched already; yet in the case of one at least of these disadvantages, the fact that a pastoral economy makes excessive demands on space, one can at once respond that all the evidence suggests that territorial space was more widely available in the Early Iron Age than at any period for many centuries on either side of it. In part, too, I think that the grounds for objection are part of a wider assumption that "sedentism" is a desired condition, and that movement of residence is to be avoided whenever possible. I was glad to find that, in his latest work, no less a figure than Lewis Binford has

attacked this assumption in print: he cites his own experience
with Australian Aborigines, Alaskan Eskimos, !Kung Bushmen,
and mobile horticulturalists in Mexico, all of whom would (and
did) strongly disagree with this proposition.[8] If it is objected that
none of these peoples were pastoralists who had abandoned an
earlier agricultural regime, then let us turn instead to historical
evidence from Central Asia. Owen Lattimore has referred to
well-attested cases of sedentary agricultural populations choosing to revert to a pastoral regime, often of a more thoroughgoing
kind than what I am positing for Greece, in that it usually involved at least seasonal mobility of habitation.[9]

A second, and to me more substantial, line of objection is that
the model of a resurgence of pastoralism is extremely hard to test
from the archaeological evidence—particularly that available
from the Greek Early Iron Age; that it lacks the elementary qualities of verifiability or falsifiability, let alone the predictive power
that we had hoped for. I do not think that this is quite true, as I
hope to show; and in general, if archaeology has not yet devised
effective criteria for distinguishing the material remains of a pastoralist culture from an agricultural one, it is high time that it did
so. As a matter of fact, one of the few recent achievements of the
new archaeology which even Paul Courbin, in his very critical
account of it, accepts is the development of the hypothesis of seasonal occupation of sites, an idea that could be of relevance to
our inquiry.[10] But this potential line of criticism must nevertheless be taken seriously.

The Early Iron Age of Greece seems to me a possible field in
which to advance and test this model because, for all the shortcomings of the archaeological record, there is as usual some nonarchaeological evidence that can be called on for independent

8. Binford (cited above, n. 2), 204.
    9. O. Lattimore, *Studies in Frontier History* (London, 1962), 246, with
references.
    10. P. Courbin, *Qu'est-ce que l'archéologie?* (Paris, 1982), 215; cf. 111–113.

support. One cannot include, under this latter heading, the many a priori assertions that the Dorians, with other alleged immigrants to central and southern Greece at the close of the Bronze Age, had a pastoral or even a nomadic background that they transplanted to their new homes. Such claims, however often repeated, simply beg all the questions. I would trace back the *scientific* attempt to substantiate such propositions to an influential article by the Swiss ethnologist Karl Meuli on the origins of the Olympic Games, published in 1941.[11] Meuli found significant correspondences between the early form of the Olympic festival and the funerary rites practiced by pastoralist tribes in Asia. From this he deduced a similar organization for the Dorian Greek society of the region of Elis, surrounding Olympia, in the early eighth century B.C. One does not need to follow Meuli all the way in his acceptance of the then universal view that these Dorians were fairly recent nomadic immigrants from further north to think that there is some validity in the correlations he observed. In particular, his linkage of the festival with *funerary* practice gains some support from the early cases of hero-cult and ancestor worship that we considered in chapter 5. We now know from direct archaeological evidence, as Meuli could not, that this type of commemorative cult was being practiced in Greece at approximately the right period: the building at Lefkandi (Figure 54), if correctly interpreted as a *hērōön*, is the earliest and most impressive case. This gives force to his claim that the games began their history as a funerary cult at the tumulus identified with the grave of the hero Pelops (Figure 59): it has since been argued in more detail that this tumulus may have been a genuine (if anonymous) prehistoric burial mound.[12] This inclines me to treat with greater respect Meuli's separate claim that the particular form of

11. K. Meuli, "Der Ursprung der Olympischen Spiele," *Die Antike* 17 (1941): 189–208.

12. H.-V. Herrmann, "Zur ältesten Geschichte von Olympia," *AM* 77 (1962): 3–34, especially 18–19.

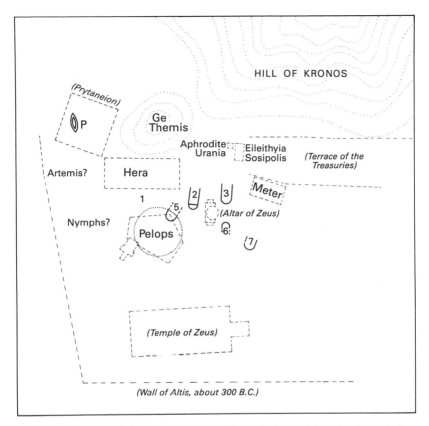

HILL OF KRONOS

(Prytaneion)

P

Ge
Themis

Aphrodite
Urania

Eileithyia
Sosipolis

(Terrace of the
Treasuries)

Artemis?

Hera

1

Meter

Nymphs?

Pelops

(Altar of Zeus)

(Temple of Zeus)

(Wall of Altis, about 300 B.C.)

Figure 59. Plan of the sanctuary at Olympia in prehistoric times (after H.-V. Herrmann).

the Olympic celebration is characteristic of pastoral herdsmen—especially since, as we shall shortly find, the western Peloponnese is one of the areas that can offer independent evidence.

A quite different line of approach was used some years later by Thalia P. Howe, who worked from the documentary evidence of the Linear B tablets on the one hand and the *Works and Days* of Hesiod on the other.[13] In the didactic nature of Hesiod's poem,

13. T. P. Howe, "Linear B and Hesiod's Breadwinners," *TAPA* 89 (1958): 44–65.

she saw a tract designed to inculcate the first principles of cultivation in an audience unfamiliar with them and cited the Mycenaean documents as evidence for the earlier prevalence of a
stock-rearing economy. It has to be conceded that this literal
reading of the instructional passages in the *Works and Days* ig-
nores the force of the didactic genre itself, which habitually
adopts such a rudimentary tone; just as some of the supporting
evidence from Homer, in addition to the problem of dating its
origins, may also be no more than a product of the heroic genre,
this time presenting a meat-based diet as the norm, but once
again out of pure convention. Further, there is much force in the
objection recently made by Paul Millett, that the *Works and Days*
contains much other material besides agricultural exhorta-
tions.[14] In my book on this period in 1971, I made use of Howe's
argument,[15] including the certainly mistaken corollary that the
supposed pastoral regime extended right back into Mycenaean
times. It is today clear that the Mycenaean economy, at any rate,
was a mixed one, in which cultivation played an important part;
so that the pastoralist phase, if real, would have to be seen in the
form in which I am now proposing it: as an interlude that began
in the post-Mycenaean age.

This revised view can still draw support from the evidence, advanced in my book, of the appearance in the ninth and eighth
centuries, for the first time since the Bronze Age, of buildings interpreted as granaries, and of small clay models of the same (Figure 60). Such evidence for the practice of intensive cultivation is
still absent from the preceding phases. But for the hypothesis to
be properly tested, fresh evidence is needed that will not merely
be compatible with the theory of an extension of pastoralism, but
positively support it. Such evidence, in my view, exists; I shall
rehearse it in the chronological order of the appearance of pub-

14. P. C. Millett, "Hesiod and His World," *PCPS* 210 (1984): 103.
15. Snodgrass, *The Dark Age of Greece* (cited above, n. 7), 378–80.

Figure 60. Restored drawing of clay model granaries from ninth-century grave in the Agora, Athens (after E. L. Smithson).

lication, taking my first espousal of the theory in 1971 as a base-date.

In 1973 Klaus Kilian published a paper arguing that the dedications of small bronzes at a sanctuary of Artemis at Pherai in Thessaly could be best explained by seasonal visits of transhumant shepherds, since the typological origin of the bronzes lay in Macedonia and further north (Figure 61).[16] This explanation at least involves a credible route of transhumance, attested in more recent times down the line of the Pindus chain and its foothills, but it is not suggested that the same factors could have operated all over the southern part of the peninsula at this time (the bronzes are primarily of eighth-century date). It would not be difficult, however, to test the interpretation at other sanctuary sites: a coherent picture of the geographical scope of this possible transhumance pattern might then emerge, strengthening the case for its reality.

In the course of a general survey of the Early Iron Age in 1975,

16. K. Kilian, "Zur eisenzeitlichen Transhumanz in Nordgriechenland," *Archäologisches Korrespondenzblatt* 3 (1973): 431–35.

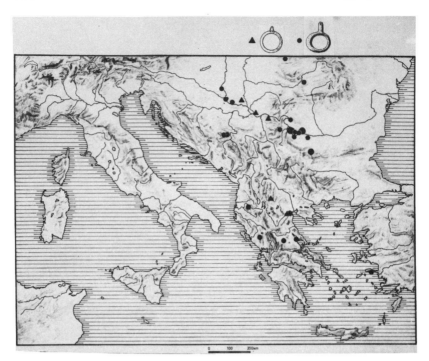

Figure 61. Distribution map of Early Iron Age ring pendants in the Balkan peninsula (after K. Kilian).

the Hungarian scholar J. Šarkady introduced a new argument.[17] He observed that of the hundreds of Mycenaean sites that were evidently deserted in at least the earlier part of the Iron Age, many were reoccupied in later times, and in some of these cases the names given to the new settlements were ancient ones: that is to say, they were the names the places had borne in Greek heroic legend, which presumably meant the historical names of the Mycenaean era. Even if oral tradition had kept alive the names as names, something more practical was needed to explain how

17. J. Šarkady, "Outlines of the Development of Greek Society in the Period Between the 12th and 8th Centuries B.C.," *Acta Antiqua Academiae Scientiarum Hungaricae* 23 (1975): 121.

the memory of the *locations* had been preserved during the centuries in which the actual sites had lain empty. Šarkady argued that intermittent visits by pastoralists would provide the necessary explanation. It may clarify his hypothesis if I give some figures, taken again from the area of Boeotia that has provided a background for our argument before. Richard Hope Simpson and Oliver Dickinson have catalogued fifty-eight Bronze Age sites from this region, of which fifty-five were occupied in Mycenaean times.[18] Just three of these can be shown to have been inhabited in the earlier part of the Iron Age, though the number rose somewhat in the ninth and eighth centuries. Later still, however, a long list of former Mycenaean sites was reoccupied, including Erythrai, Kreusis, Anthedon, Thespiai, Eutresis, Siphai, Thisbe, Chorsiai, Medeon, Koroneia, and Chaironeia. We may be able to give these places their proper ancient names today, but how do we know they already bore them in the Mycenaean period? Philological arguments could be applied in some cases, but a more general argument is that several of these places are mentioned in Greek legend, and M. P. Nilsson's work has taught us to respect the Mycenaean pedigree of "heroic geography."[19] It is also very much to the point that a number of these place-names occur in the Catalogue of Ships in the second book of the *Iliad*, which in many opinions reinforces their claim to have kept their names from at least the end of the Mycenaean period. Yet in the interval nearly all of them underwent a period of three centuries or more of apparent desertion (sometimes, as at Eutresis, even longer).

Next, there is some evidence of a strictly archaeological kind.

18. R. Hope Simpson and O. Dickinson, *A Gazetteer of Aegean Civilisation in the Bronze Age* (Göteborg, 1979), 221–24 (nos. F59–F66, including F64A) and 235–54 (nos. G1–7, G9–31, G33–47, including G40A). These were all occupied in Mycenaean times, but only G10, G23, and perhaps G22 have produced Submycenaean or earlier Protogeometric pottery.

19. See, especially, M. P. Nilsson, *The Mycenaean Origin of Greek Mythology* (Berkeley, 1932), 100–136 on Boeotia.

In 1978, for the first and, so far, the only time, a collection of animal bones from an excavated Early Iron Age site was published; predictably, the site was Nichoria.[20] It was possible to make a comparison between this faunal evidence and the comparable material from the earlier, Mycenaean levels at the same site. In the opinion of the experts who published it, the evidence allowed of a clear conclusion: the use of domesticated species at Nichoria showed first an upsurge in the proportion of cattle in the Early Iron Age; and second, a concomitant change in the ages at which cattle, sheep, and goats were slaughtered. These changes are to be explained by a major shift to stock-rearing, with the ranching of beef cattle as its chief component.

It might well be asked at this point whether direct *structural* evidence of short-term occupation should not be forthcoming if a stock-rearing population was in existence and was intermittently changing its places of residence as I have suggested. In 1981 evidence of this kind was discovered in the course of the Greco-Swiss excavation of the earliest levels at Eretria, belonging perhaps to the very beginning of the eighth century.[21] Here, underlying the apsidal houses of the later Geometric period, there emerged a series of outlines of circular huts, founded on a simple bedding of mixed sand and clay, and embedded in the virgin sand of the foreshore; the walls, of which fragments survived, had been of *pisé* (Figure 62). These were clearly ephemeral structures, and their position underneath the earliest permanent houses precludes an explanation of them as temporary builders' quarters. The excavators interpret them as seasonal huts, occupied by

20. R. E. Sloan and M. A. Duncan, "Zooarchaeology of Nichoria," in *Excavations at Nichoria in Southwest Greece*, vol. 1, ed. G. Rapp and S. E. Aschenbrenner (Minneapolis, 1978), 60–77.

21. L. Kahil, "Erétrie à l'époque géometrique," *Annuario* 59 (1981): 165–73, especially 167–68 (with discussion, 345–46); and more briefly "Quartier des maisons géometriques," *Ant. K.* 24 (1981): 55–56, comparing M. R. Popham, L. H. Sackett, and P. G. Themelis, *Lefkandi*, vol. 1, *The Iron Age* (London, 1979–80), 16, pl. 8b.

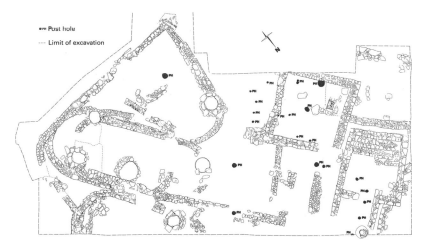

Figure 62. Part of the 1981 excavation area at Eretria, Euboea (after L. Kahil).

short-term visitors before the decision to found a permanent settlement had been taken; they also point to a parallel, of comparable date, in the curvilinear structures underlying the Geometric houses at nearby Lefkandi. The degree of short-term commitment to a site is compatible with, and perhaps best explained by, seasonal visits for pasturage. In the same vein, an entire settlement of this period, but of a very different kind and in a contrasting location, has now been interpreted by its excavator as a seasonal base for a community of transhumant pastoralists: this is Vitsa Zagoriou, in the mountains of Epirus.[22] The evidence consists not only in the high altitude of the site above sea level, making winter occupation barely tolerable, but also in the prevalence of bones of cattle, sheep, and goats all over the site. Once again, the proximity to the known transhumance route of the Pindus chain makes this a persuasive interpretation, though its implications need not extend very far geographically.

22. J. P. Vokotopoulou, "Ē Ēpeiros ston 8° kai 7° aiōna p. Chr.," *Annuario* 60 (1982): 89.

A quite different kind of claim, a priori in nature but none the less testable, was advanced by Michel Sakellariou in a 1980 book, and then extended in its scope at a later conference.[23] We have noted several times the prevalence of the apsidal plan of house on the Greek mainland in the Early Iron Age: Sakellariou suggests that this house shape can be more generally associated with mobile pastoralists; if the claim can be substantiated, it would of course have very far-reaching implications. In a similar spirit of generalization, the veteran historian and geographer Ernst Kirsten has put forward the suggestion that another feature of the material culture of this period, which we have not yet mentioned, the increasing incidence of handmade pottery of fairly high quality, might be explained as the product of mobile pastoral communities who did not enjoy regular access to a potter's wheel.[24] This again could easily be dismissed as an unsubstantiated conjecture, but the phenomenon that it seeks to interpret is nevertheless a real one, which has found no other satisfactory explanation.

We have seen that the only body of evidence from animal bones of this period has proved to give positive support to our hypothesis. Another class of organic material that could be expected to be of help in this context is that of seeds; and in 1982 Glynis Jones published the first analysis of well-dated seed remains of this period, from the Early Iron Age settlement levels at Iolkos in Thessaly.[25] Once again, the results are coherent and,

23. M. B. Sakellariou, *Les Proto-Grecs* (Athens, 1980), 118–26, with his discussion intervention in *Annuario* 59 (1981): 345.

24. E. Kirsten, "Gebirghirtentum und Sesshaftigkeit," in *Griechenland, die Ägäis und die Levante während die "Dark Ages"*, Symposion Zwettl, ed. S. Deger-Jalkotzy (Vienna, 1983), 437 n. 64.

25. G. Jones, "Cereal and Pulse Remains from Protogeometric and Geometric Iolkos, Thessaly," *Anthropologika* 3 (1982): 75–78. Nichoria too had previously produced seed evidence—see J. M. and C. T. Shay, "Modern Vegetation and Fossil Plant Remains," in *Excavations at Nichoria*, vol. 1 (cited above, n. 20), 41–59—but it is very sparsely distributed among the chronological periods there.

from our point of view, arguably positive. From the floor levels of a building of Protogeometric (eleventh to tenth centuries B.C.) date, a deposit consisting almost entirely of pulse seeds was recovered; from a later floor, of Geometric date, the remains consisted largely of carbonized grain seeds. There is thus a clear contrast between the two periods and, inasmuch as the pulse could most plausibly be explained as animal fodder, the apparent sequence conforms to the picture of an initial concentration on stock-rearing and a later resurgence of cultivation that is posited by our hypothesis.

I should like to end by adding a particle of new evidence of my own. Since sanctuary deposits are, for the later part of the Greek Early Iron Age, so clearly the richest archaeological source, it occurred to me to try to exploit their evidence in some way, and the dedications of animal figurines at Olympia seemed to offer an opportunity.[26] Olympia is perhaps the richest site in this sphere, and as the Early Iron Age approached its end, the sanctuary began to attract offerings from a wide area of the Peloponnese, and even beyond; during the Archaic period, however, the animal dedications die out. Between the tenth and the eighth centuries B.C., the proportion of oxen and sheep among these figurines, initially very high, shows a steady decline, although the ox figurines in particular (Figure 63) remain very numerous. If we isolate dedications believed to come from beyond the immediate region of Olympia (in most cases, they are in the style of the northeastern Peloponnese), then the proportion of oxen and sheep shows a steeper decline, until they vanish altogether (Figure 64). The interpretation of these figures is not free of problems: the residue of the dedications, which shows a corresponding increase over the years, is primarily made up of horse figurines, a type that is probably without relevance to farming practice. But the change

26. The figures that follow are based on the catalogues in W.-D. Heilmeyer, *Frühe Olympische Tonfiguren* and *Frühe Olympische Bronzefiguren*, Olympische Forschungen, nos. 7 and 12 (Berlin, 1972 and 1979).

Figure 63. Typical ox figurines dedicated at Olympia.

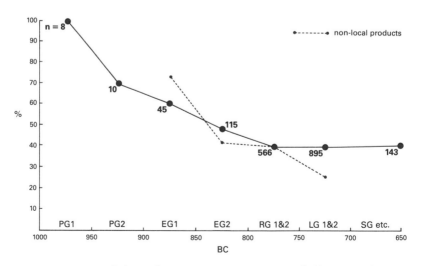

Figure 64. Ox and sheep figurines as a percentage of all animal figurine dedications at Olympia.

over time is at least compatible with the idea that from the tenth century B.C. to the seventh, oxen and sheep had a role of diminishing importance in the life of the communities making the dedications; and that this diminution was more rapid in an area outside the immediate vicinity of Olympia, the northeastern Peloponnese. That the ox figurines reflect a concern with herding, rather than with the use of this animal for plough traction, is admittedly an assumption; but in the light of their large numbers, their close association with sheep and rams, and their general appearance of being beef cattle, it does seem the likeliest one. At any rate, there is nothing to contradict our hypothesis that the peak in livestock farming occurred in the earlier part of the Iron Age, and that a falling-off occurred with the approach of the historical period.

This survey of the findings of the past twelve years has not been a selective one: I have included all the evidence known to me that has a clear bearing on the issue. However one judges it in other respects, the new evidence unquestionably has the quality of independence of the initial hypothesis, since it was unknown at the time when that was formed. It includes at least six instances of entirely fresh material—the Thessalian bronzes, the Nichoria bones, the hut foundations at Eretria and Lefkandi, the evidence from Vitsa, the Iolkos seeds, and the Olympia animal figurines—that at the least are compatible with the original hypothesis, and in some cases may be thought positively to support it. Nothing that is directly contradictory has, to my knowledge, come to light during this same period.

All of this, however, makes only a fragmentary beginning to the task of validating the initial hypothesis. Now that they have already emerged, it is too late to put forward this list of findings as being predictable or deducible from the original "pastoralist model." Yet they do suggest that that model is, up to a certain point, a testable one; and it can now be predicted that further replications of them will give similar results. This may appear to fall far short of David Clarke's prescription for archaeological synthesis, from which we started out; but I would still claim that the model of increased pastoralism in the Early Iron Age of Greece possesses a certain explanatory force.

Let us recall the problem that we originally posed ourselves: that of explaining the long duration of the material conditions of the Early Iron Age, as attested in the archaeological record. If, as I have suggested, Greek communities at this period were collectively devoting more of their resources to stock-rearing than before or afterwards, then this would be a clear case of adaptation to changed conditions. The breakdown of the Mycenaean palace system must have thrown the pattern of landownership into turmoil; the apparent desertion of many sites is likely to have brought with it the neglect of the agricultural land surrounding them; the experience of internal migrations over a period of several generations probably discouraged everybody from too close an attachment to the land. To practice large-scale stock-rearing from a few fixed bases could have seemed a perfectly reasonable response to such circumstances; and it would also go some way towards explaining the archaeological record of this time.

That record is characterized by an apparent absence of centralized control and of signs of major collective action; and later, after about the mid eleventh century B.C., by a prolonged lack of significant innovation of any kind. The relative lack of urgency of the pastoral way of life, and the readiness to move one's place of residence rather than struggle to consolidate, would conform to that picture; it would account for the otherwise surprising persistence of the elements that compose the picture; and, what is more, it would explain the most remarkable feature of the *historical* evidence for this period—its virtual nonexistence. What may have seemed to contemporaries an acceptable solution to their problems may well have held little or no interest for later generations of Greeks, who were by then otherwise occupied.

I shall end with a more precise restatement of the hypothesis of Early Iron Age pastoralism, refined to some degree by the findings of recent years that have been discussed. I suggest that over much of central and southern Greece, widely spaced, sedentary communities supported themselves in part by cultivation of the adjacent land, but also, to a far greater extent than earlier or later, by pastoral use of the more or less empty spaces that had opened up in the map of Greece. In some restricted areas to the north, as is suggested by the evidence from Pherai and Vitsa, some of them may have practiced actual seasonal transhumance.[27] In the western Peloponnese, there are signs—from the Nichoria bones and the Olympia dedications—that cattle ranching may have been the most prominent form of pastoral activity. When the drive to reassert the supremacy of cultivation brought its inevitable tensions, some of its supporters probably used the larger settlements as bases from which to extend plowing. Others, also preferring a nonpastoral way of life, may have formed the settlers for the new island communities that feature so prominently in the archaeological record between about 900 and 700 B.C. Gradually, this new order came to prevail, and found its fulfillment in the remarkable explosion of Greek culture that took place in the later eighth century and afterwards, bringing with it the territorially based city-state of historical Greece.

A plea for greater attention to be paid by the archaeologist of Greece to the approaches and insights of nonclassical archaeology, and conversely for the nonclassical archaeologist to become more aware of the potential the Greek field offers; a warning of the incommensurate nature of true archaeology and traditional,

27. For a partial parallel to the case argued here, but based on the distribution of a pottery ware of a very much earlier period in Greece, see T. W. Jacobsen, "Seasonal Pastoralism in Southern Greece: A Consideration of the Ecology of Neolithic Urfirnis Pottery," in *Pots and Potters*, ed. P. M. Rice (Los Angeles, 1984), 27–43.

event-oriented history; an urgent summons to attend to the archaeology of the Greek landscape, despite or even because of the relative neglect of this sector by the ancient sources; a suggestion for exploiting the opportunities for integrating historical studies of ancient art with archaeological and other evidence; an attempt to apply different interpretative methods to a notoriously problematic episode in the development of Greek civilization—what do these efforts add up to? They are, I think, something more than the airing of a series of personal prejudices. They have in common the purpose of advocating a modest degree of change, whereby a perhaps uniquely conservative discipline could modify and extend its field without sacrificing the true strengths that have kept it alive hitherto.

References for the Illustrations

(Figures 11, 12, 14, 21, 23, 24, 30, 46, 47, 52, 54, 62, and 64 were redrawn by John Parsons, Eureka Cartography, Berkeley.)

1. W. Dörpfeld, *Alt-Ithaka* (1927), Tafel 10.
2. Ibid., Beilage 22.
3. Ibid., Beilage 31.
4. A. Mallwitz and W. Schiering, Olympische Forschungen, no. 5 (1964), 6, Abbildung 2, courtesy of Prof. Dr. A. Mallwitz and the Deutsches Archäologisches Institut, Athens.
5. Ibid., Tafel 64, courtesy of Prof. Dr. W. Schiering and the Deutsches Archäologisches Institut, Athens.
6. W.-D. Heilmeyer, *Archäologischer Anzeiger* 1981, 448, Abbildung 4 (DaI Athen, neg. Ol.7264), courtesy of Prof. Dr. W.-D. Heilmeyer and the Deutsches Archäologisches Institut, Athens.
7. E. Buchner, *Die Sonnenuhr des Augustus* (1982) 60–61, Abbildung 1, courtesy of Prof. Dr. Edmund Buchner.
8. *Die Sonnenuhr des Augustus*, Tafel 129, courtesy of Prof. Dr. E. Buchner.
9. *Die Sonnenuhr des Augustus*, Tafel 141, courtesy of Prof. Dr. E. Buchner.
10. Drawing by Michael J. Moore from D. J. Breeze, *The Northern Frontiers of Roman Britain* (1982), 104, fig. 22, courtesy of Dr. David J. Breeze.
11. Map showing sites of selected Western Greek colonies.
12. M. R. Popham, L. H. Sackett, and P. G. Themelis, *Lefkandi*, vol. 1 (1979–80), pl. 4, courtesy of Mervyn R. Popham.

13. Courtesy of the City Art Gallery, Manchester, England.
14. H. A. Forbes, "Strategies and Soils: Technology, Production and Environment in the Peninsula of Methana, Greece" (Ph.D. diss., University of Pennsylvania, 1982), 149, courtesy of Dr. Hamish A. Forbes.
15. After W. Kiepert, *Formae Orbis Antiqui* (1906), pl. xiv.
16. Author's drawing.
17. After N. Bergier, *Histoire des grands chemins de l'empire romain*, vol. 2 (1728), segment 5.
18. Author's drawing.
19. Photograph by J. L. Bintliff.
20. Photograph by J. L. Bintliff.
21. J. F. Cherry, in *Archaeological Survey in the Mediterranean Area*, ed. D. W. Rupp and D. Keller (1983), 410, fig. 1, courtesy Dr. John F. Cherry.
22. J. L. Bintliff and A. M. Snodgrass, *Journal of Field Archaeology* 12 (1985): 126, fig. 1.
23. *Journal of Field Archaeology* 12 (1985): 128, fig. 2.
24. Drawing after *Journal of Field Archaeology* 12 (1985): 137, fig. 12.
25, 26, 27, 28. *Journal of Field Archaeology* 12 (1985): 138, fig. 13; 140, fig. 16; 146, fig. 19; 148, fig. 22.
29. *Journal of Field Archaeology* 12 (1985): 135, fig. 9.
30. Drawing after author's map.
31, 32, 33, 34. Author's photographs.
35. Boston 99.518, Painter of the Boston Polyphemos, *ABV* 198, courtesy Museum of Fine Arts, Boston.
36. Paris, Cab. Méd. 190, Rider Painter, courtesy Bibliothèque Nationale, Paris.
37, 38. Antikenmuseum Basel und Sammlung Ludwig inv. no. BS 498, Antimenes Painter, courtesy Antikenmuseum Basel und Sammlung Ludwig and Prof. Dr. Margot Schmidt.
39. Paris, Louvre A 517, photograph Hirmer-Fotoarchiv, courtesy Musée du Louvre, Paris.
40. Paris, Louvre A 519, after E. Pottier, *Vases antiques du Louvre*, vol. 1 (1897), pl. 20.
41. Copenhagen NM 1628, photograph National Museum, Copenhagen.
42. Athens NM 4310, E. T. Vermeule, *Aspects of Death in Early Greek*

Art and Poetry (1979) 17, fig. 10, courtesy National Museum, Athens, and Prof. Emily Vermeule.

43. Corinth Museum, M. C. and C. A. Roebuck, *Hesperia* 24 (1955), pl. 63, courtesy American School of Classical Studies, Athens.
44. Copenhagen 727, photograph National Museum, Copenhagen.
45. Athens, Agora P 4885, projected drawing by Piet de Jong, courtesy American School of Classical Studies, Athens.
46. Author's drawing.
47. C. W. Blegen, *Prosymna* (1937), plan 5.
48. London, British Museum 1899.2–19.1, B. Schweitzer, *Greek Geometric Art* (1971), pl. 72, courtesy Trustees of the British Museum.
49. Oxford 1938.1129, photograph Ashmolean Museum, Oxford.
50. Athens NM 6209, photograph National Museum, Athens.
51. G. Phylaktopoulos and C. Bastias, *History of the Hellenic World*, vol. 1 (1974), 271, courtesy Ekdotikē Athinōn S.A.
52. Drawing after author's *The Dark Age of Greece* (1971), 366, fig. 113.
53. M. R. Popham, L. H. Sackett, and P. G. Themelis, *Lefkandi*, vol. 1 (1979–80), pl. 244, photograph Mervyn R. Popham.
54. Drawing M. R. Popham, updated from *Antiquity* 56 (1982): 170, fig. 2, courtesy Peter Calligas and Mervyn R. Popham.
55. W. Kraiker, *Kerameikos*, vol. 1 (1939), Tafel 2, photograph Deutsches Archäologisches Institut, Athens.
56. W. A. McDonald et al., *Excavations at Nichoria in Southwest Greece*, vol. 3 (1983), 37, fig. 2-23, courtesy Prof. William D. E. Coulson.
57. W.-D. Heilmeyer, *Frühgriechische Kunst* (1982), 98, fig. 82, courtesy Prof. Dr. W.-D. Heilmeyer and Gebr. Mann Verlag, Berlin.
58. W.-D. Heilmeyer, *Frühgriechische Kunst* (1982), 95, fig. 80, courtesy Prof. Dr. W.-D. Heilmeyer and Gebr. Mann Verlag, Berlin.
59. Drawing H.-V. Herrmann, updated from *AM* 77 (1962): 16, Abbildung 2, courtesy Prof. Dr. H.-V. Herrmann.
60. E. L. Smithson, *Hesperia* 37 (1968), pl. 27, no. 23, courtesy Prof. Evelyn Smithson and the American School of Classical Studies, Athens.
61. K. Kilian, *Prähistorische Zeitschrift* 50 (1975), Tafel 91, courtesy Prof. Dr. Klaus Kilian.
62. L. Kahil, in C. Krause, *Antike Kunst* 24 (1981): 85, fig. 9, courtesy Vereinigung der Freunde Antiker Kunst and Prof. Lily Kahil.

63. W.-D. Heilmeyer, Olympische Forschungen, no. 12 (1979), Tafel 94 (DaI Athen, neg. Ol.4441), courtesy Prof. Dr. W.-D. Heilmeyer and the Deutsches Archäologisches Institut, Athens.
64. Drawing after author's original.

Index

Designer:	Laurie Anderson
Compositor:	Wilsted & Taylor
Text:	Sabon
Display:	Trump
Printer:	Malloy Lithographing
Binder:	Malloy Lithographing